Faithlore

Faithlore
The Invented Reality

John Fulling Crosby

RESOURCE *Publications* · Eugene, Oregon

FAITHLORE
The Invented Reality

Copyright © 2018 John Fulling Crosby. All rights reserved. Except for brief quotations in critical publications or reviews, no part of this book may be reproduced in any manner without prior written permission from the publisher. Write: Permissions, Wipf and Stock Publishers, 199 W. 8th Ave., Suite 3, Eugene, OR 97401.

Resource Publications
An Imprint of Wipf and Stock Publishers
199 W. 8th Ave., Suite 3
Eugene, OR 97401

www.wipfandstock.com

PAPERBACK ISBN: 978-1-5326-5318-6
HARDCOVER ISBN: 978-1-5326-5319-3
EBOOK ISBN: 978-1-5326-5320-9

New Revised Standard Version Bible, copyright 1989, Division of Christian Education of the National Council of the Churches of Christ in the United States of America. Used by permission. All rights reserved.

Manufactured in the U.S.A. 06/12/18

This book is for questers, skeptics, humanists, freethinkers, doubters, and all those who cannot accept canned theological answers to life's great questions. Some of these folk are Christians in the traditional sense of the word. Others are churchgoers who feel restless and somewhat compromised. For eleven years, I dwelt among and preached to this latter group. They were, for the most part, enjoyable to be with, mostly because they were not shirtsleeve Christians, but seekers of truth. To them and their kin, I dedicate this work.

I want to thank Joe Lee, Michael Shermis, Rob Hongen, and Sandy Dolby for their stalwart support, ranging from ideas to expertise to art. And thanks to the Humanist/Freethinkers of the Unitarian Church of Bloomington, Indiana for their ongoing encouragement.

Contents

Preface I: Revealed Theology Versus Natural Theology | ix

Preface II: A Forenote on Hermeneutics, the Principles of Interpretation | xi

Introduction: Faithlore Reality | xiii

1. Who Was the Historical Jesus? | 1
2. What Did Jesus Do? | 18
3. Myth, Folklore, and Faithlore | 30
4. Constructivism and the Human Brain | 46

Conclusion | 64

Appendix I: Need Theory | 67

Appendix II: American Civil Religion | 71

Appendix III: Cosmological Evolution and Descent of Sapiens | 75

Bibliography | 79

Preface I
Revealed Theology Versus Natural Theology

Of first order is the necessity to separate by definition authoritative or "revealed" religious traditions from so-called "natural" religions, or religions arising out of natural expressions of plant, animal, and human life and nature as part and parcel of all creation, including the cosmos of both micro (quanta) and macro. An appeal to nature and/or to the forces of nature, including worship of the sun and the rhythms of our solar system and the galaxies of the universe (deism), is not to be equated with a godhead or god force that foreordains every human being into a personal I-Thou relationship with itself. Another way of saying this is to say simply that theism presupposes personal and intimate relationship between the theistic Godhead/Creator and the creature into which this God has breathed the *ruach*, or the breath of life (Gen 2:07; 6:17; 2 Sam 22:16).[1]

Traditionally, Christian theism is both immanent and transcendent. Historically speaking, deism is usually defined as being transcendent only, not immanent. Deism has been the dominant theology espoused by William Paley.[2] Spinoza's pantheism (God is All) and panentheism (God is in All) may be considered philosophical offshoots of deism and modern expressions of spiritualism

1. All Scripture references in this book are from the NRSV.
2. Paley, *Natural Theology*.

In contrast with natural theology, revealed or authoritarian/authoritative theology claims that God, Yahweh, Elohim, or Allah is the omnipotent and omniscient almighty force transcending the universe. Through revelation, the god force has revealed, and continues to reveal, its divine intention for all humankind (or at least to the faithful who seek to know its will).

Throughout these pages, the underlying question is this: to what extent are we justified in making the claim that nearly all religious or theological language is folkloric in nature, especially claims regarding Christian theistic propositions? Is there any empirical evidence, other than personal religious experience (anecdotal),[3] that claims theism to be both valid and true? In short, is there any evidence to the contrary; i.e., is there any evidence that theism is not folklore, faithlore, or lore?

---

3. James, "Varieties of Religious Experience."

Preface II
A Forenote on Hermeneutics, the Principles of Interpretation

Hermeneutics is the art and science of interpretation, most usually the principles of interpretation involved in the interpretation of the sixty-six books of the Christian bible. Hermeneutic principles include, but are not necessarily limited to, literal interpretation, liberal interpretation, anagogical (mystical) interpretation, neo-orthodox interpretation, moral, allegorical, feminist interpretation, historical interpretation, LGBT interpretation (lesbian-gay-bisexual-transgender), mythological, and folkloric interpretation.

Traditionally, the hermeneutic is only one part of biblical translation. Exegesis, in tandem with hermeneutics, is the dominant and necessary art and science of textual translation and textual criticism. Exegesis includes the higher (or historical) criticism and the lower (or textual) criticism. The lower criticism includes spelling, grammar, sentence construction, word choice, word organization, and flow.

Introduction: Faithlore Reality

Never would I have dreamed, kneeling before fifteen or so Presbyterian ministers in June of 1956 at my ordination as they laid their hands on my head, that one day I would rise up and claim that the belief system in which I was being ordained was lore. "Faithlore," as a play on the word "folklore," is still lore. Usually, but not always, it is not factual truth, nor is it usually connected in any manner with so-called empirical truth. Whether it is emotional or spiritual truth depends on the frame of mind of the believer.

Lore is based on myth. Myth is often based on wishful thinking. I grew up thinking this way (unconsciously) all throughout my philosophy major at Denison University and theological degree at Princeton Theological Seminary—and then on into eleven years as a minister and pastor. In the tenth year, my wishful thinking came crashing down into a swamp of useless pretense.[4] Nevertheless, in my final year of ministry, Jesus still remained somewhat of an exemplar to me.

I concluded that Jesus' god was nothing more than the creation or invention of Jesus' own mind. Jesus' own faith was lore. And if lore was an invention of Jesus' mind, I certainly could now accept that I had allowed Jesus' lore to become my lore. Lore was an invention of my creative *sapiens* brain, entirely capable of dominating my thought.

---

4. Crosby, *Aftermath*; see also Crosby, *Flipside of Godspeak*.

The intervening fifty years as a university professor and marriage/family therapist have been good to me, and I have been fortunate to grow old along with my wife and our three sons. Nevertheless, the former life never completely left me, inasmuch as I did not have the intellect to deal with my apostasy or my loss of faith. In short, I was never successful in bringing closure to my earlier life. That is, until I realized that my brain was the product of acquired intellectual acumen giving rise to my imagination. I created this god. I invented it. I worked on it until I was sure I had it right! I had long accepted this Kerygma, this Christian belief system, as myth, but never had I clearly seen the interaction of myth with my creative imagination. It all seems so simple now! I simply failed to see how much of my original faith was anchored in the lore of how I wanted reality to be.

In these pages, I have shared how my personal faithlore and the idea of Jesus being an exemplar came about. I concluded that faithlore was an invention of my imagination, perhaps a figment! Albert Schweitzer helped me. So did David Friedrich Strauss, Bart Ehrman, David Eagleman, Yuval Harari, Andrew Newberg, Ernst von Glassersfeld, and Paul Watzlawick. But finally, I take responsibility for my faithloric conclusion.

1 Who Was the Historical Jesus?

Who Was Jesus of Nazareth?

This little volume will outline two major domains of biblical thought that are absolutely necessary for a foundation in studies about Jesus. Who was Jesus and what did he do? (chapters 1 and 2). Additionally, we must address the role of myth and folklore, as these impact what people come to believe as tenets of faith (chapters 3 and 4).

First we must address the following question: who was Jesus of Nazareth? By way of answer, we shall turn to the classic work of Albert Schweitzer, *The Quest of the Historical Jesus*. This is a late-nineteenth-century–early-twentieth-century work. There are also second-, third-, and fourth-quest endeavors, with several modern contributions. We must start, however, with Schweitzer's classic contribution to the literature.[1]

It would be so much easier if all we needed to do was read the four Gospels. Unfortunately the four Gospels don't tell us nearly as much as we need to know. They were written between ca. 70 CE and 110 CE by men who ascribed their work to Matthew, Mark, Luke, or John. They each wrote from a different viewpoint or perspective. Mark was a lot like a reporter who wrote with little

1. Schweitzer, *Quest of the Historical Jesus*. For a complete overview of the question of whether or not Jesus actually lived, see Cooke: "Poor scholarship, aggressive/ defenses styles of arguing, and extravagant conclusions are not new to current mythicist scholarship . . . the recent reemergence of the theory can be seen as its fifth incarnation" ("Myth Theory," 7).

elaboration. Matthew and Luke, however, were storytellers. Matthew was telling his version of the story to Jews. Luke was telling his version to gentiles. Alternatively, John was probably writing his version of events to Greeks. John was less like a reporter or a storyteller, and more like a poet.

I hesitate to say this, but it even makes a difference which version or translation of the New Testament a person uses. Not all scholars agree on the meaning of the Greek words. Jesus spoke Aramaic. This makes translation even more difficult.[2]

There has always been, and evidently will be for a long time to come, people who desire (even demand) the following: 1) that the so-called written Word of God—that is, the sixty-six books of the Old and New Testaments—be held as containing the divinely inspired Word of God, even to the point of believing that God directed the point of the pen; 2) that these books are forever held as being absolutely inerrant, i.e., without error; these two doctrinal tenets of faith held by (practically) all Christian fundamentalists, in spite of the knowledge of ancient languages combined with the disciplines of the higher (historical) criticism and the lower (textual) criticism, reflect not simply a stubbornness to reason, but a preference to dwell in the land of sheer ignorance.

As a result of the Enlightenment, which took place throughout Europe and England (especially in Germany) in the sixteenth, seventeenth, eighteenth, and nineteenth centuries, literally hundreds of scholars began to investigate the Bible in both literary and historical ways. Theology was not neglected, but it slowly took a backseat to historical investigation.

---

2. I primarily use the New Revised Standard Version of the Bible with Apocrypha (published by the Council of the Churches of Christ in the USA). My own Greek and Hebrew is quite rusty, so I rely heavily on footnote references within the text. Also, I should note that a translation is usually the work of an individual. A version is usually a large body of scholars acting at the behest of a church or a denomination, or even a king. For example, the King James Version of the Bible was authorized by King James of England. It is dated at 1611 CE. King James did not write it. Noted scholars and churchmen of the day were appointed to the task.

1 WHO WAS THE HISTORICAL JESUS?

Until the enlightenment, Christendom clung to the doctrines and creeds of the church. After the Nicene Creed and its offspring, the Apostles' Creed, there reigned supreme among theologians and church fathers the Definition of Chalcedon. Chalcedon (451 CE) attempted to define and describe, once and forever, the relationship between the earthly Jesus and the heavenly Christ—that is, the substantive makeup of the human Jesus versus the divine Christ.

> Therefore, following the holy Fathers, we all with one accord teach men to acknowledge one and the same Son, our Lord Jesus Christ, at once complete in godhead and complete in manhood, truly God and truly man, consisting also of a reasonable soul and body; of one substance [ὁμοούσιος] with the Father as regards his Godhead, and at the same time of one substance with us as regards his manhood.[3]

Approaches to the Historical Backdrop: Super Naturalistic-Rationalistic/Spiritualistic-Mythological

With the publications of the first "Lives of Jesus," there burst forth a wealth of conjecture and scholarship never before known to humankind. In the wake of the predominant supernaturalists came the rationalists. I include with the rationalists the spiritualists, who attempted to put a spiritual take on the miracles, including the healings, the resurrections, and the water, fish, and feeding episodes.

A third approach to the Jesus narratives, following the supernaturalists and the rationalists, was the way of David Friedrich Strauss. According to modern scholar Bart D. Ehrman,

> The supernatural interpretation can't explain the text and the natural explanation ignores the text. According to Strauss, both modes of interpretation err precisely because both of them see the story as a historical account.

---

3. Bettenson, *Documents*, 73.

In fact, Jesus' walking on the water is not an actual historical event but a myth—a history-like story that is trying to convey a truth.[4]

Strauss developed the concept of the myth. We must understand the word "myth" as having several meanings. Following Strauss, we understand that myth, while being untrue in a literal sense, may be a vehicle for the conveyance of truth. We consider fairy tales to be myths because they often convey deep truth. This emphasis on myth would get Strauss into a lot of trouble. Nevertheless, his work remains seminal.

This third category, in addition to the supernaturalists and the rationalists, contains many "Lives of Jesus." Ehrman states,

> One thing has remained constant since Strauss. There continue to be scholars—for most of this century, it's been the vast majority of critical scholars—who think that he [Strauss] was right, not in all or even most of the specific things he said, but in the general view he propounded.[5]

Before we look further at these three, let us look briefly at another tribe or school of scholars. I call them the apocalyptics because they bring out into the open the questions to which I referred earlier. Who was Jesus? What was his understanding of himself? What did the Messiah mean to Jesus? Was his Messianic ambition his own view of the Messiah, or the traditional Jewish view of the Messiah? Was Jesus the Son of Man? What does "Son of Man" mean or imply? And perhaps most crucial of all, what was meant by the "kingdom of God"? Was it a future paradise in eternity, or was it a present possibility for those following Jesus?

Increasingly, in the study of the lives of Jesus we face the question of Jesus and his belief in the last times, the *echaton* facing the demise of the world. As things worked out, Schweitzer's *Quest of the Historical Jesus* essentially ended the quest. It would take two world wars and a revival of faith in the "living Christ" before

---

4. Ehrman, *Jesus: Apocalyptic Prophet*, 29.
5. Ehrman, *Jesus: Apocalyptic Prophet*, 30.

1 WHO WAS THE HISTORICAL JESUS?

there would be a renewed interest in the historical Jesus. In the neo-liberal and neo-orthodox periods, personages such as Karl Barth, Rudolph Bultmann, Emile Brunner, Reinhold and Richard Niebuhr, and Paul Tillich dominated the theological scene. Additionally, there were Harry Emerson Fosdick and Norman Vincent Peale, neither of whom were neo-orthodox, but both of whom were ultra liberal in their hermeneutics, their theory and method of interpretation.

Seventy Lives of Jesus in the Nineteenth Century: Schweitzer's Attempt to Make Sense of the Quest

Each "Life of Jesus" had some powerful effect on its author.

> Reimarus evaded that woe by keeping the offence to himself and preserving silence during his lifetime—his work, "The Aims of Jesus and His Disciples," was only published after his death by Lessing. But in the case of Strauss, who, as a young man of twenty-seven, cast the offence openly in the face of the world, the woe fulfilled itself. His "Life of Jesus" was his ruin.[6]

There is a literary Jesus, a synoptic Jesus, an eschatological Jesus, a Messianic Jesus, a Son-of-Man Jesus, and, for our purpose, a historical Jesus. There are implicit problems with all of them. The best place to begin is to attempt to give answer to the question, how did Jesus think of himself?

1. Did he define himself as the Messiah? If so, in what sense? The Jewish view of Messianic reality was of political and military predominance. The Messiah is not one who would suffer and be crucified and buried in a cave. Emphatically, the Jesus of history did not conform to the Jewish idea of Messiahship. Did Jesus think of himself as the suffering servant of Isaiah? If so, this was quite foreign to the Jewish idea of stately, political, and religious stature. The Jewish Messianic

---

6. Schweitzer, *Quest of the Historical Jesus*, 5.

vision was absolutely foreign to the suffering servant of Isaiah as developed in Isaiah 52:13-53—53:1-12.

2. Did Jesus think of himself as the Son of Man? The Son of Man idea emanates from the Old Testament book of Daniel: "To him was given dominion and glory and kingdom . . . one like a son of man" (7:1-14). Was the Son of Man a metaphor for the deliverer of Israel? Did Jesus adopt this term in reference to himself?

3. What about the kingdom of God? There is no question that Jesus taught about the coming of the kingdom. Was the kingdom a place or a state of mind in which one commands and conducts oneself to be always under God's rule? Or, was the kingdom the product of the eschatological end-times? Of course, not everyone would be admitted to the future kingdom. Only those who survived the final judgment. Jesus taught about the coming Messiah and the Son of Man, but he always stopped short of self-identification with these concepts. There is little question that his favorite oratorical theme was the kingdom of God. The question remains, did Jesus actually identify himself as being the incarnation of the concepts about which he taught?

4. We must also note that the evidence, both internal (biblical) and external (including the Apocrypha, the Gospel of Thomas, the Gospel of Peter, the Dead Sea Scrolls, and personages such as Pliny the Younger, Tacitus, and Josephus) almost always points not to a full lifetime of Jesus, but rather only to his two-to-three years of teaching, healing, and public ministry.

The truth is, in terms of historical veracity, we know very little about the life of Jesus. The seventy "lives of Jesus" reflect, according to Schweitzer, not only the different epochs of time, but also the various points of view of the individual researchers. This is to say, if Professor x is a rationalist or spiritualist, he/she will come up with a rationalistic or spiritualistic Jesus. If Professor y is one who believes in the millennium, he/she will somehow find a

1 WHO WAS THE HISTORICAL JESUS?

Jesus who believes in the coming of the millennium. If Researcher z is an apocalyptic personage, he/she will somehow end up with an apocalyptic Jesus. Schweitzer says, "There is no historical task which so reveals a man's true self as the writing of a life of Jesus."[7] He also comments that:

> The critical study of the life of Jesus has been for theology a school of honesty. The world has never seen before, and will never see again, a struggle for truth so full of pain and renunciation as that of which the Lives of Jesus of the last hundred years contain the cryptic record.[8]

If this conclusion by Schweitzer is accurate, then we have an excellent illustration of how constructivism works![9] In truth, each researcher, from Reimarus to Paulus to Strauss, has constructed the version of Jesus his scholarship has led him to see and to create. The work of deconstruction includes the study of each individual who has endeavored to write a life of Jesus. Who is he? (Yes, they were all men.) What is his background? What is his life story? What shade of theological assumptions tended to color his hermeneutic, his interpretation of the events and sayings of Jesus?

Reimarus, Paulus, and Strauss

Reimarus was not published until after his death. Paulus, the second of our noted scholars, was denied several academic positions and stripped of others. Strauss, perhaps the greatest of the scholars, was practically run out of town.

Herman Samuel Reimarus (1694–1768) wrote seven fragments. Today we call them essays.

> To say that the fragment on "The Aims of Jesus and His disciples" is a magnificent piece of work is barely to do it

---

7. Schweitzer, *Quest of the Historical Jesus*, 4.
8. Schweitzer, *Quest of the Historical Jesus*, 5.
9. Glasersfeld, *Radical Constructivism*. Constructivism does not deny the reality of the objective world, but it claims that all humans grasp reality via the functioning of the human brain.

justice. This essay is not only one of the greatest events in the history of criticism, it is also a masterpiece of general literature.[10]

Reimarus was a deist and a rationalist. He did not believe in miracles. Reimarus believed Jesus to be a product of his time who believed in the Jewish expectation of a forthcoming Messiah. Jesus was absolutely human. Reimarus portrayed Jesus as one who spoke forth about the kingdom of God being at hand: "Repent, for the Kingdom of Heaven is at hand" (Matt 3:2). Baptism and the Lord's Supper must not be interpreted as meaning there is a new religion.

> Baptism in the name of Jesus signified only that Jesus was the Messiah . . . for the only change which the teaching of Jesus made in their [the Jews'] religion was that whereas they had formerly believed in a Deliverer of Israel who was to come in the future, they now believed in a Deliverer who was already present.[11]

According to Reimarus, Jesus fully expected people to respond to his message about the kingdom of God being fulfilled in himself, e.g., Jesus, the Messiah.

Heinrich Paulus (1761–1851) was a thoroughgoing rationalist. Every miracle ascribed to Jesus, including the feeding of the five thousand, the walking on the water, and his resurrection from the dead can be explained. Many miracles are ascribed to simple misunderstandings. Everybody followed the lead of Jesus and his disciples, who shared their food with each other. This served as an invitation for the crowd to also share their baskets of food. The boat failed to go very far out in the water because the wind was blowing inward toward shore. Jesus was wading as he tried to help Peter get back in the boat. The resurrection didn't really happen because Jesus was not really dead.

When I was a student at Princeton Seminary (1953–1956), I often found myself trying to explain the miracles by coming up

---

10. Schweitzer, *Quest of the Historical Jesus*, 15.
11. Schweitzer, *Quest of the Historical Jesus*, 18.

with explanations such as those rendered by Paulus. In bull sessions with other students, I seemed to be the loner. Like Paulus of old, I believed that Jesus was only a man. He was human. My own time in the pastoral-preaching ministry was devoted to this type of interpretation. My goal was to help bring the carpenter, the son of Joseph and the leader of men, to life in the eyes and hearts of my congregants. I tried to be completely rational in my approach to the miracles, especially in matters pertaining to the alleged virgin birth and the resurrection. I would attempt to spiritualize that which I could not otherwise explain. Healing miracles seemed to give me more latitude than other types of miracles. I dwelt heavily on the parables and teachings of Jesus, always concerned with making the scene and the situation come alive. I certainly neglected (ignored) the apocalyptic Jesus messages and behaviors. I always celebrated the Jesus who reputedly gave us the Sermon on the Mount.

According to Paulus, Jesus seemed to work miracles only because people did not fully comprehend his movements and his ability to help people gain perspective and resolution of their dilemmas. Jesus sometimes used the power of suggestion. Sometimes, according to Paulus, Jesus used medicines known only to him: "The truly miraculous thing about Jesus is himself, the purity and supreme holiness of His character, which is, not withstanding, genuinely human, and adapted to the imitation and emulation of mankind."[12]

Schweitzer says that, for Paulus, the question of miracles can neither be overthrown nor attested as truth, and that everything that happens in nature emanates from the omnipotence of God.[13] In short, Paulus refused to accept miracles at face value. One way or another, everything could be explained away. To Paulus, believing was seeing. People believed what they thought they saw and saw what they believed. Paulus, according to Schweitzer, was a fully developed and thoroughgoing rationalist. According to Schweitzer, the rationalistic approach by Paulus to the study of the life of Jesus was destroyed by Strauss.

12. Schweitzer, *Quest of the Historical Jesus*, 51.
13. Schweitzer, *Quest of the Historical Jesus*, 51.

FAITHLORE

David Friedrich Strauss (1808–1874) is heralded by many scholars, including Schweitzer, as being the central figure in the quest of the historical Jesus. In short, he is the myth scholar, because myth is the method by which he retains the integrity of the teachings of the historical Jesus, protecting and defending Jesus' teachings and physical actions before the crowds of adoring admirers. (I would here interject, for the sake of the reader in attempting to better understand the twenty-first-century meaning of the word "myth," that we perhaps can grasp Strauss's intended meaning by using the phrase "legendary myth.") It is, for Strauss, myth-based or grounded in legend. Strauss did not intend to tie myth to untruth, but rather to legendary truth.

Schweitzer claims,

> Considered as a literary work, Strauss' [sic] first Life of Jesus is one of the most perfect things in the whole range of learned literature . . . Myth formed . . . the lofty gateways at the entrance to, and at the exit from, the Gospel history; between these two lofty gateways lay the narrow and crooked streets of the naturalistic explanation.[14]

Prior to Strauss, myth had been used in Old Testament interpretation, but not in New Testament exegesis or hermeneutic. Strauss reminds his readers that there were no eyewitness reports regarding the sayings, teachings, and movements of Jesus. Nothing was written down at the time of events and episodic happenings.

Schweitzer describes Strauss's method thusly:

> The supernaturalistic explanation of the events of the life of Jesus had been followed by the rationalistic, the one making everything supernatural, the other setting itself to make all the events intelligible as natural occurences. Each had said all that it had to say. From their opposition now arises a new solution—the mythological interpretation. This is a characteristic example of the Hegelian method—the *synthesis* of a *thesis* represented by the supernaturalistic explanation with the *antithesis* represented by the rationalistic interpretation . . . Each

---

14. Schweitzer, *Quest of the Historical Jesus*, 78.

1 WHO WAS THE HISTORICAL JESUS?

> incident of the life of Jesus is considered separately; first as supernaturally explained, and then as rationalistically explained, and the one explanation is refuted by the other ... in these Strauss recognises only the last desperate efforts to make the past present and to conceive the inconceivable; ... he sets up the hypothesis that these inexplicable elements are mythical.[15]

As an example of Strauss's use of legendary mythology, let us now consider the reputed conception of Jesus in the womb of Mary by the Holy Spirit.

- Matthew 1:21–23: "An angel of the Lord appeared to him in a dream and said, 'Joseph, son of David, do not be afraid to take Mary as your wife, for the child conceived in her is from the Holy Spirit. She will bear a son and you are to name him Jesus, for he will save his people from their sins.' All this took place to fulfill what had been spoken by the Lord through the prophet: 'Look, the virgin shall conceive and bear a son, and they shall name him Emmanuel,' which means 'God is with us.'"

- Isaiah 7:14: "The Lord himself will give you a sign. Look, the young woman [Hebrew *almah*, "young woman"; Greek *parthenos*, "virgin"] is with child and shall bear a son, and shall name him Immanuel ["God with us"].

Strauss comments:

> In the world of mythology many great men had extraordinary births, and were sons of the gods. Jesus himself spoke of his heavenly origin, and called God his father; besides, his title as Messiah was—Son of God ... In conformity [with the passages above] the belief prevailed that Jesus, as the Messiah, should be born of a virgin by means of divine agency ... But according to historical truth, Jesus was the offspring of an ordinary marriage, between Joseph and Mary; an explanation which, it has

---

15. Schweitzer, *Quest of the Historical Jesus*, 80–81.

been justly remarked, maintains at once the dignity of Jesus and the respect due to his mother.[16]

> It was . . . a common notion among the Jews . . . that the Holy Spirit co-operated in the conception of pious individuals; moreover, that God's choicest instruments were conceived by divine assistance of parents, who could not have had a child according to the natural course of things. And if, according to the believed representation, the extinct capability on both sides was renewed by divine intervention (Rom 4:19), it was only one step further to the belief that in the case of the conception of the most distinguished of all God's agents, the Messiah, the total absence of participation on the one side was compensated by a more complete superadded capability on the other . . . thus must it have appeared to the author of Luke [Luke 1:37, for nothing will be impossible with God], since he dissipates Mary's doubts by the same reply with which Jehovah repelled Sara's incredulity. Neither the Jewish reverence for marriage, nor the prevalent representation of the Messiah as a human being, could prevent the advance to this climax; to which, on the other hand, the ascetic estimation of celibacy, and the idea, derived from Daniel, of the Christ as a superhuman being, contributed.[17]

Strauss develops his mythus, on the order of the above, throughout the entire synoptic narratives, dealing laboriously with almost every episode involving Jesus. Schweitzer's summation runs as follows:

> In the stories prior to the baptism, everything is myth. The narratives are woven on the pattern of Old Testament prototypes, with modifications due to Messianic or messianically interpreted passages. Since Jesus and the Baptist came into contact with one another later, it is felt necessary to represent their parents as having been connected. The attempts to construct Davidic genealogies for Jesus, show us that there was a period in

---

16. Strauss, *Life of Jesus*, 140–41.
17. Strauss, *Life of Jesus*, 141.

1 WHO WAS THE HISTORICAL JESUS?

the formation of the Gospel History during which the Lord was simply regarded as the son of Joseph and Mary, otherwise genealogical studies of this kind would not have been undertaken. Even in the story of the twelve-year-old Jesus in the temple, there is scarcely more than a trace of historical material.[18]

The above quotation from Schweitzer serves as an excellent example of Strauss's methodology. In his entire book, Strauss allows us to see the supernaturalistic explanation, as well as the rationalistic explanation prior to his development of the mythus.

The Jesus Seminar: Funk and Hoover

The most notable event in the modern quest for the historical Jesus is the creation of *The Jesus Seminar* and its sponsoring agency, the Westar Institute. Led by Robert W. Funk and Roy W. Hoover, its noteworthy publication is *The Five Gospels: What did Jesus Really Say?*[19] This work from 1993 is a search for the authentic words of Jesus, with over one hundred participating New Testament scholars actually voting according to a four-point scale on the likelihood of Jesus speaking or saying the words of a sentence, phrase, or paragraph. One of the three dedicatees is David Friedrich Strauss!

The authors take the view that John the Baptist, not Jesus, was the true eschatological/apocalyptic figure. Funk and Hoover claim that in the seventies and eighties, scholars were free from the neo-orthodoxy of Karl Barth and the idea of an eschatological Jesus. "John the Baptist, not Jesus, was the chief advocate of an impending cataclysm, a view that Jesus' first disciples had acquired from the Baptist movement."[20] Funk and Hoover state that "Jesus himself then rejected that mentality in its crass form, quit the ascetic desert, and returned to urban Galilee." Jesus' new point of view was characterized by the parables and his emphasis on God's imperial rule.[21]

18. Schweitzer, *Quest of the Historical Jesus*, 81.
19. Funk and Hoover, *Five Gospels*, 4.
20. Funk and Hoover, *Five Gospels*, 4.
21. Funk and Hoover, *Five Gospels*.

Jesus' followers did not grasp the subtleties of his [Jesus'] position and reverted, once Jesus was not there to remind them, to the view that they learned from John the Baptist. As a consequence of this reversion, and in the aura of the emerging view of Jesus as a cult figure analogous to others in the Hellenistic mystery religions, the gospel writers overlaid the tradition of sayings and parables with their own memories of Jesus. They constructed their memories out of common lore, drawn in large part from the Greek Bible, the message of John the Baptist, and their own emerging convictions about Jesus as the expected messiah—the Anointed.[22]

The Apocalyptic Prophet: Bart Ehrman

Bart Ehrman published *Jesus: Apocalyptic Prophet of the New Millennium* in 1999. This work stands today as a landmark study because it considers all of the Jesus material—that is, all of his parables, warnings, prognostications, teachings about the kingdom of God, healing episodes, fishing episodes, and feeding episodes. Ehrman does not utilize the methodology of the Jesus Seminar (that is, attempting to judge the authenticity of material that may or may not "sound" like something Jesus would or would not have said).

As with the primary contributors to the Jesus Seminar, Ehrman is free of denominational or creedal ties and affiliations. He writes from the perspective of sound New Testament scholarship, carefully tracing the lexical roots of the Jesus material, and his bibliography is instructive for all New Testament endeavors.

Ehrman is emphatically not in the supernaturalist camp, nor is he in the rationalist-naturalist sphere of influence. He does not identify with Strauss's views concerning the mythus, or what I have called legendary myth. Further, he does not agree with Funk and Hoover regarding Jesus' alleged breaking away from the teachings of John the Baptist and his apocalyptic message.

---

22. Funk and Hoover, *Five Gospels*, 4.

1 WHO WAS THE HISTORICAL JESUS?

In Ehrman's view, there is no other viable explanation for Jesus' teachings and interventions than as an apocalyptic prophet who believed in the imminent coming of the end times.

> The historical Jesus did not teach about his own divinity or pass on to his disciples the doctrines that later came to be embodied in the Nicene Creed. His concerns were those of a first-century Jewish apocalypticist. Jesus anticipated that the end of the age was coming within his own generation. God would soon send a cosmic judge from heaven to right all the wrongs of this world, to overthrow the wicked and oppressive powers that opposed both God and his people, to bring in a perfect kingdom in which there would be no more hatred, war, disease, calamity, despair, sin, or death. People needed to repent in view of this coming day of judgment, for it was almost here . . . It's no wonder that a figurative [naturalistic, rationalistic, legendary myth] construal of Jesus' words became so popular so soon and achieved such dominance for so long. If Jesus were to be taken literally—that is, if he really meant that the Son of Man was to arrive in the lifetime of his disciples—he was obviously wrong.[23]

If Ehrman is correct in his analysis, and I personally believe he is closer to the truth than most scholars are willing to admit, then we can probably infer that Jesus was but one of many would-be prophets and apocalyptics of his day. It was not unusual for vagabonds and other homeless men to become wandering prophets, forthtellers of a future judgment and eschaton. While there can be little doubt about the reality of a strong legendary mythology enveloping the person of Jesus, the essential driving thrust of Jesus' core message remains rooted in his first-century conviction that the day of judgment was soon to be a reality, and the kingdom of God was soon to be established.

---

23. Ehrman, *Jesus: Apocalyptic Prophet*, 243–44.

Coda

In the final pages of *The Quest of the Historical Jesus*, it sounds as if Dr. Schweitzer is reverting to the Christ of faith, or the Jesus of faith, compared to the Jesus of history. At best, he sounds as if the impossibility of recovering a true Jesus of history compels a continuing devotion to the Jesus of faith.

In these remarks, I think it best that we allow Dr. Schweitzer to speak for himself.

> Jesus means something to our world because a mighty spiritual force streams forth from Him and flows through our time also. This fact can neither be shaken nor confirmed by any historical discovery. It is the solid foundation of Christianity.
>
> The mistake was to suppose that Jesus could come to mean more to our time by entering into it as a man like ourselves. That is not possible. First because such a Jesus never existed. Secondly because, although historical knowledge can no doubt introduce greater clearness into an existing spiritual life, it cannot call spiritual life into existence. History can destroy the present; it can reconcile the present with the past; can even to a certain extent transport the present into the past; but to contribute to the making of the present is not given unto it.[24]

But the truth is, it is not Jesus as historically known, but Jesus as spiritually arisen within men, who is significant for our time and can help it. It is not the historical Jesus, but the spirit that goes forth from him and strives in the spirits of men for new influence and rule, which overcomes the world.[25]

This last paragraph is troubling to many followers of Schweitzer because it sounds as though he is retreating to the Christ of faith, a spiritualized position void of attachment and connection to the Jesus of history.

As for me, if all I can really know is an apocalyptic Jesus, then count me out! I have no need to construct or to reconstruct a

---

24. Schweitzer, *Quest of the Historical Jesus*, 397.
25. Schweitzer, *Quest of the Historical Jesus*, 399.

1 WHO WAS THE HISTORICAL JESUS?

Christ of faith or a Jesus of faith. Jesus was a man of his time. His historical context is well-recorded.[26] I have no doubt or reservation about labeling him a prophet (Greek "to speak forth," "to tell forth"). I think present-day scholarship as summarized by Bart Ehrman regarding the apocalyptic prophet is trustworthy; that is to say, both reliable and valid.

To what extent the Jesus of history (chapter 1) can be constructed as the Christ of faith (chapter 2) I leave to the reader to determine for themselves. One thing is certain: in deconstructing Jesus, we are freed from the belief, according to Saint Paul, that underlies the Christian tradition. This belief, "if Christ has not been raised, then our proclamation has been in vain and your faith has been in vain," emphatically does not underlie the Christian tradition. The plain and simple reason for this is that if there were no human Jesus, there could have been no life or death of Jesus. I hold, contrary to Saint Paul, that the only belief that underlies the Christian tradition is the fact of Jesus' life.

While I am free from Saint Paul's belief, I hold strongly to the belief that the Jesus of history has made a great impact on human history, even unto the relations between nations and amongst peoples. I hold to this day that, in spite of the fact that I left the Presbyterian ministry, my life is immeasurably richer for having believed in this man.

The fact of radical deconstruction of the Jesus of history gives valid basis for the belief that the Christ of faith is an illusion, a theological construct created by would-be believers. The alleged prophetic/apocalyptic Jesus of history, for better or for worse, remains the legacy bequeathed to us by the historical Jesus.

---

26. Also see: Ehrman, *Did Jesus Exist?*.

2 What Did Jesus Do?

Our second challenge is to address the question about the Christ of faith. Many refer to the Christ of faith as the Living Lord or just "the Lord." For countless Christian believers, the Jesus of history is unimportant; instead, for them, the salient issue is to ask the question of "What has Jesus done for you?" In other words, it is not the person of Jesus that is important, but the saving work that he performed. Or, as others would have it, "the saving work of God accomplished through Jesus." In chapter 1, I relied on the time-honored work by Albert Schweitzer, *The Quest of the Historical Jesus*.[1] I also relied on the more recent scholarship of Bart Ehrman, author of *Jesus: Apocalyptic Prophet of the New Millennium*.[2] I am futher indebted to T. W. Manson, who contributed greatly to our understanding of the teachings of Jesus.[3] In chapter 2, I have relied heavily on the work of L. W. Grinstead in *A Short History of the Doctrine of the Atonement* in my review of atonement theory.[4]

I will also be relying on myself. I dedicated my life to the ministry of Jesus until I was thirty-six years old.[5] Now, fifty years

1. Schweitzer, *Quest of the Historical Jesus*. Also see Strauss, *Life of Jesus*.
2. Ehrman, *Jesus: Apocalyptic Prophet*.
3. Manson, *Teaching of Jesus*.
4. Grinstead, *Short History*.
5. My path to that point is traced as follows: Princeton Theological Seminary, 1953–1956; associate minister, First Congregational Church in Saginaw, MI, 1956–1958; organizing and first minister, Westlake Presbyterian Church in Battle Creek, MI, 1958–1962; minister, First Presbyterian Church in

2 WHAT DID JESUS DO?

later, at age eighty-six, I am ready to share my answers as to who Jesus was and what he did. If you do not wish to do the work of exploring and reading, then be advised ahead of time about who Jesus was and what he did not do. In short:

Jesus was a common man who believed in a father god to the point of allowing himself to be put to death for his belief. His most widely accepted body of teaching is the so-called Sermon on the Mount (Matt 5:1—7:29; also called the Sermon on the Plain in Luke 6:17–49).

We come now to the second major question(s). What did Jesus actually do? Did he build a church? Did he provide for the forgiveness of your so-called sins? Did he provide for you to ascend into heaven when you die? Did he sanctify you (make you holy or clean or sanctified)? Did he somehow satisfy God's desire to punish all the people's of the world, interceding in our behalf at God's bar of justice? Did he appease God's wrath and anger, as one who intervenes at court in behalf of the accused? Did he enter into battle with the devil and demonic forces so as to defeat them once and for all? Did he provide a means for the ongoing judgment of this world, its governments, its institutions, its industries, and its economic, agricultural, and its energy systems? Did he pave the way for all the peoples and nations of the world to live in peace? Some say that yes, he did all of these things.

Or, following the Jesus of chapter 1, did he simply walk among us, approaching us on our roadsides, in our offices, fields of labor, automobiles, living rooms, bedrooms, restaurants, drama stages, theaters, movie houses, soccer fields, football stadiums, basketball arenas, brothels, sex worker haunts, public baths, and private emporiums? Do we encounter him at NATO or the United Nations, at Walmart or Amazon, in the Silicon Valley, at Fox News, ESPN, or MSNBC? (Or even the White House?)

Some say that if he did not do the works of atonement, he could not be the Messiah or the Son of God.

What if you were to say that you could not identify with the Jesus figure of chapter 1, but that the Jesus of chapter 2 was your

---

Baldwinsville, NY, 1962–1967.

kind of Jesus? Today, it is the more conservative folk who hold to the Jesus of chapter 2, and it is the less doctrinal, more liberal among us who hold to the ever-present non-doctrinal Jesus of chapter 1. "After all," these liberals proclaim, "if Jesus does not continue to live and walk and dwell amongst us in the dens and stores and assembly lines of our everyday lives, then there is no point in any atonement or religious ceremony or folderol."

Let us look more closely at the New Testament and Old Testament ideas of what Jesus is reputed to have accomplished in his short time here on earth. Here follows a short description of the saving works of Jesus, as depicted by theologians since the second century after the birth of Christ. There are other theories, but they appear to be knockoffs of these first five. Be warned that these are not really theories in any modern philosophical or scientific sense, but merely suggested explanations of how the life, death, and alleged resurrection of Jesus has contributed to the so-called salvation of humankind.

I. The Ransom Theory

The definition of ransom is the redeeming or release of a captive or of seized property by payment of money or compliance with other demands, according to *Webster's New World College Dictionary* (3rd edition). First Corinthians 6:19–20 and 7:23 say that we are not our own; we were bought with a price. Matthew 20:28 similarly states that "the son of man came not to be served but to serve, and to give his life as a ransom for many."

Ever since Adam disobeyed God and ate of the fruit of the tree of the knowledge of good and evil he, along with Eve, and all the descendants of Adam and Eve, have been under the power of the devil. This devil (or Satan, or Lucifer, by these or any other names) now owns and controls all humankind.

The only way God can get mankind back from the clutches of the devil is for God to pay the devil a ransom (this is surely a sign of God's lack of omnipotence). Evidently, the ransom the devil demanded was that God's beloved Son would have to be crucified. And there we have it. God gave his Son to death on the cross in the fulfillment of the terms of the ransom as laid out by the devil. In other words, God paid off the devil by allowing Jesus to be put to death. Of course, according to this theory, God would have the last laugh because God would raise Jesus from the dead.

The early church father involved in this theory is Origen, as per Grinstead: "The comparative paucity of ideas as to the atonement in earlier writers is more than made good when we come to Origen, the greatest and most many-sided theologian of the first three centuries."[6]

Grinstead states,

> From man's point of view, though not necessarily from the point of view of God, the devil was in just possession. He had a right to name his price for the release of man. The price demanded was the blood of Christ, and this price was paid . . . He released man, only to discover that he has no power over the soul of Jesus which he had accepted in exchange.[7]

The ransom theory is still popular amongst those who perceive a so-called living devil. Yet, as a theory, it has waned, especially among those moderns who refuse to believe in Satan or satanic involvement with Jesus the son or God the father. In some ways, this is difficult to understand inasmuch as modern followers of the penal substitutionary theory, most popular since the time of John Calvin, often end up with the ransom idea; that is, because of Adam's transgression in the garden of Eden, all of Adam's descendants stand condemned unless/until Jesus gives his own earthly existence as a sacrifice.

---

6. Grinstead, *Short History*, 61.
7. Grinstead, *Short History*, 38.

II. The Christus Victor Theory
(Literally, Christ the Victor)

The Christus Victor theory is very close to the ransom theory. Gustaf Aulen, a Swedish theologian of the nineteenth century, is its primary advocate.[8] The terminology implies "warfare," "friend," "foe," "victor," and "vanquished." If there is a victor, there must be a vanquished foe. Christ is victorious over the powers of death and the powers of Satan.

This is a theory of retributive justice wherein God rules the universe according to strict rules of retribution. Sin of any kind must be paid for by somebody or something. The sinner must be redeemed. The sin must be overcome, defeated, wiped away.

Martin Luther's great reformation hymn, "A Mighty Fortress Is Our God," reflects the battle between God and Satan.

> A mighty fortress is our God,
> A bulwark never failing:
> Our helper He, amid the flood
> Of mortal ills prevailing.
> For still our ancient for
> Doth seek to work us woe;
> His craft and power are great,
> And armed with cruel hate,
> On earth is not his equal.
> Did we in our own strength confide,
> Our striving would be losing;
> Were not the right Man on our side,
> The Man of God's own choosing.
> Dost ask what that may be?
> Christ Jesus, it is he;
> Lord Sabaoth is his name,
> From age to age the same,
> And He must win the battle.
> And though this world, with devils filled,

---

8. Aulen, *Christus Victor*.

Should threaten to undo us,
We shall not fear, for God hath willed
His truth to triumph through us.
The Prince of Darkness grim—
We tremble not for him;
His rage we can endure,
For lo! His doom is sure—
One little word shall fell him.[9]

III. The Satisfaction Theory

The prime spokesperson for this theory was Anselm, Archbishop of Canterbury (1033–1109).

Who wants satisfaction? God? Jesus? Lucifer? Satisfaction for what? The primary problem is to satisfy the justice of God. God was in a bind. Jesus was sinless (Heb 4:15), so he did not have to die. All mankind is "in sin" and hence cannot pay its own debt ("the wages of sin is death," Rom 6:23). In God's eyes, sin is a debt that can be balanced or satisfied only by payment from a sinless person. The satisfaction theory demands that God's sense of justice be satisfied by the erasure of accumulated debt. *Dakia* (Greek for justice) demands payment. The only person or agency capable of payment is Jesus, the Sinless Son of God. Therefore, Jesus' death on the cross serves to absolve all who put their trust in Christ. The debt owed to God is satisfied; that is, paid in full.

> Let us consider whether God could properly remit sin by mercy alone without satisfaction—to remit sin would be simply to abstain from punishing it. And since the only possible way of correcting sin, for which no satisfaction has been made, is to punish it, to not punish is to remit it uncorrected. But God cannot properly leave anything uncorrected in his kingdom.[10]

---

9. Luther, "Mighty Fortress."
10. Bettenson, *Documents of the Christian Church*, 192–95.

In legal terms, if a person is pronounced guilty by a jury or judge, he/she may be subject to one of the following alternatives:

a. Go to jail or prison to await execution.

b. Go to jail or prison for a designated period of time.

c. Be pardoned by legal authority after having served some or all of the required sentence.

d. Be released from custody, the sentence having been commuted. Commutation means that the felon is not pardoned, but the unfulfilled part of the original sentence is forgiven or simply cancelled. (Time served is deemed sufficient in terms of punishment.)

e. Be the beneficiary of a sentence now expunged from the books of court. A verdict expunged is a verdict deemed never to have happened.

In summary, the satisfaction theory directs its logic toward the internal consistency of God's justice. God's justice is satisfied and fulfilled.

IV. The Penal Substitution Theory

In the penal substitution theory, God punishes sinful humankind for the original sin stemming from Adam's fall from grace (that is, Adam's disobedience to God's command that "you may freely eat of every tree of the garden; but of the tree of the knowledge of good and evil you shall not eat, for in the day you shall eat of it you shall die" in Genesis 2:15–17).

According to this theory, all humankind deserves to die because we are all Adam's descendants. Who or what can possibly override this verdict? Who or what can override the punishment due each of us because we are human and stand in Adam's progeny? The answer is that Jesus, who was sinless, took upon himself the punishment due each of us. Jesus serves the punishment due each of us, hence penal substitution.

This theoretical line of reasoning is the most modern of all atonement theory. It is the result of the Calvinism of the protestant reformation. Further, the penal substitution theory easily became the favorite atonement theory for clergy who attended bible schools or were uneducated, who seemed to favor the simplistic reasoning that Jesus died for you. This means that Jesus allowed himself to be put to death on the cross so that your sin of disobedience could be forgiven by God the father. Of course, this forgiveness and salvation was not automatic—you still had to repent of your sin. Nevertheless, a strong preacher (often known or described as a "thumper") could often persuade the congregant of their sinful nature, convicting them with a severe sense of guilt and thus bringing about the act of repentance. John Calvin spoke to this. Calvin was a highly educated scholar who had read the law and prepared himself for a legal career. Nevertheless, the principles of the Protestant Reformation seemed to take hold of him, and he became a lecturer and noted scholar in Reformation circles, especially in Geneva, Switzerland.

> Therefore original sin is seen to be an hereditary depravity and corruption of our nature, diffused into all parts of the soul . . . [For] those who have defined original sin as the lack of the original righteousness with which we should have been endowed, no doubt include, by implication, the whole fact of the matter, but they have not fully expressed the positive energy of this sin. For our nature is not merely berift of good, but it is so productive of every kind of evil that it cannot be inactive.[11]

V. The Moral Influence Theory, or Exemplar Theory

There are other variations of atonement theory. The four that have been covered so far are the most basic and most commonly treated in the literature. However, the theory many call the oldest, the so-called moral influence theory, yet remains. The moral influence

---

11. Calvin, *Institutes of the Christian Religion*. See Bettensen, *Documents of the Christian Church*, 298.

theory centers on the life, teachings, and everyday behavior of Jesus. Peter Abelard, Immanuel Kant, and Paul Tillich are reputed to have been high on this theory.

Henceforth, I shall call it the exemplar theory because it casts the man Jesus as an example worthy of our emulation. This emulation is not to be construed as a force summoning us to walk, with Jesus, the Good Friday path to the crucifixion (such as the Stations of the Cross), but perhaps as a beacon emanating from a lighthouse, pointing us to the breakwaters of protected harbors in the matter of daily living, or to a series of roadmaps marking favored routes and dangerous construction zones.

This theory (or this explanation of atonement, as we should say) attracted attention before the age of the church fathers; that is, before Apollinarius, Origen, Athanasius, Tertullian, Anselm, Augustine, Ignatius, Arius, Pelagius, Tertullian, Dionysius, Luther, or Calvin. Grinstead associates moral theory as "rectoral," or having to do with the governmental theory or the idea of God running the earth as a function of moral law.[12]

Does the exemplar theory imply that Jesus is to be our example? Yes and no. Yes, in the sense that his key teaching is about the kingdom of God being within oneself and not in some far off place and time, and no in the sense of direct imitation. Webster derives the word "exemplar" as coming from the Latin *exemplum*, "a pattern or example; a person or thing as worthy of imitation; a model, pattern, or archetype."[13]

A seminary student once railed at me that he was not a "Jesus Junior." Actually, this was a fair statement (put-down) inasmuch as the idea of being an example can be easily misunderstood or otherwise exaggerated. In our usage, "exemplar" has to do with one who stands out by the example of what true humanity and compassion is all about. As such, we emphasize words and phrases such as "empathy" over "sympathy," "caring behavior" over "condescending behavior," "giving" over "patronizing," "listening" over "talking" or "lecturing," and "engaging" over "demonstrative

12. Grinstead, *Short History*, 83.
13. *Webster's New World College Dictionary* (3rd edition).

2 WHAT DID JESUS DO?

instruction." A good friend once suggested to me the phrase "God's breakthrough." This implies characteristics such as respect, courtesy, kindness, and humility, never boastful arrogance.

Perhaps one way we can get at the meaning of "exemplar" is to ask the following of each parable, metaphor, and instructional gem: What was Jesus saying? What was his purpose, his intention, his hopeful response in terms of the listener's behavior? What did Jesus mean when he said "Go and do likewise"? The word "exemplar" intends to convey a sharing of what it means to be "of God" with humanity. This is what the humanity of God would look like, were the kingdom of God given total jurisdiction over the life of human beings.

Friedrich Schleiermacher perhaps stands as the all-time champion of the moral theory, i.e., who I have called the Exemplar. Schleiermacher rejects the Christus Victor theory, the ransom theory, the satisfaction theory, and the penal-substitution theory of atonement. Schleiermacher holds to the exemplar idea because Jesus gave himself totally and completely to unity with the Godhead. Thus, atonement is a human accomplishment resulting from a mindset that is internally and externally in tune with Jesus' way of thinking and being.

One could argue that Schleiermacher's Jesus is without grace inasmuch as atonement is a matter of human endeavor. As such, this stands in opposition to each of the other God-driven theories where some action or intervention by God is necessary for atonement to take place. In a sense, then, we may say that Schleiermacher does not reflect the Reformation doctrine of justification by grace through faith, since atonement is entirely up to the human individual.

Keith Clements, editor of *Friedrich Schleiermacher: Pioneer of Modern Theology*, states:

> The obvious starting-point in any treatment of Schleiermacher's theology is his analysis of religious 'feeling'. We then move on to his criterion for the distinctiveness of the Christian religion, seen in christocentric terms . . . In

> Schleiermacher . . . religion as feeling is emphatically primary, and theology secondary.[14]

In his "Distinctiveness of Christianity; Redemption Through Jesus Christ," Schleiermacher boldly declares:

> To participate in the Christian communion means to seek in Christ's institution an approximation to the above-described state of absolute facility and constancy of religious emotions. No one can wish to belong to the Christian Church on any other ground. But since each can only enter through a free resolve of his own, this must be preceded by the certainty that the influence of Christ puts an end to the state of being in need of redemption, and produces that other state; and this certainty is just faith in Christ.[15]

The feeling to which Schleiermacher subscribes is precisely the feeling so devoutly ascribed to by modern evangelists and preachers. It is a feeling of exhilaration at being totally caught up in a created reality of forgiveness, acceptance, and sanctification.[16]

Another modern representative of the exemplar is Horace Bushnell.

> It would not be true to say that Bushnell wholly ignores the Godward, juridical, aspects of Atonement, but he quite explicitly assigns to them a secondary position. The great primary truth is the change wrought in the heart of man, by what he terms the "moral power" of God.[17]

Grinstead, in referring to Bushnell's moral theory, states:

> It is clear that we have here the Moral theory in one of its purist forms. The mysticism of Schleiermacher has been repudiated utterly, though many traces of its influence

---

14. Clements, *Friedrich Schleiermacher*, 35.

15. Clements, *Friedrich Schleiermacher*, 115–16.

16. For a recent description of the evangelical preaching which is designed for the achievement of this response in the penitent worshipper see Barker, *Godless*.

17. Grinstead, *Short History*, 341.

remain ... Thus the death of Christ is regarded as having exactly the same purpose as His life. It was one great manifestation of perfect holiness, perfect obedience, perfect fellowship with God. And by that manifestation sin was condemned. It could not stand in the presence of the light.[18]

Some advocates of the moral theory claim that the hymn *When I Survey The Wondrous Cross* describes quite well the meaning and intent of the moral theory. This hymn was written by Isaac Watts in 1707.

> When I survey the wondrous cross
> On which the Prince of Glory died,
> My richest gain I count but loss,
> And pour contempt on all my pride
>
> Forbid it, Lord, that I should boast,
> Save in the death of Christ my God;
> All the vain things that charm me most,
> I sacrifice them to his blood.
>
> See from his head, his hands, his feet,
> Sorrow and love flow mingled down!
> Did e'er such love and sorrow meet?
> Or thorns compose so rich a crown?
>
> Were the whole realm of nature mine,
> That were a present far too small;
> Love so amazing, so divine,
> Demands my soul, my life, my all.[19]

---

18. Grinstead, *Short History*, 336.
19. Watts, *When I Survey*.

3 Myth, Folklore, and Faithlore

How Does Myth Become Faithlore?

Let us begin the discussion of lore by pointing out that lore can be true or false, historically accurate or inaccurate. Ted Williams possesses the all-time highest baseball batting average (.344). This is baseball lore. It is also true. In addition, Bob Feller was one of the fastest baseball pitchers of all time. This is baseball lore. It is also true. Past and present college football powers include Michigan, Alabama, Oklahoma, Florida, Nebraska, and Miami. Similarly, professional football powers include the New England Patriots, the New York Giants, and the Chicago Bears. All of this is lore. So far, all of this is true. Some of this is perhaps also a matter of opinion and personal belief.

Merriam-Webster says that lore is something that is taught and something that is learned, as well as knowledge gained through study or experience. Another definition says that lore is traditional knowledge or belief, a particular body of knowledge or tradition.[1]

What is the definition of folklore, including myth, legend, and the role of "lore"? To what extent are scholars, students, and even practitioners of folklore justified in referring to religion in general and theism in particular as belonging to the realm of dogma rather than to lore? What is the role of myth and lore within the pages of the Hebraic writings of the Pentateuch, the Prophets, the Hagiographa of the Hebraic Bible, and the Christian New Testament?

---

1. *Merriam-Webster's Collegiate Dictionary: Eleventh Edition.*

3 MYTH, FOLKLORE, AND FAITHLORE

This chapter contains ten illustrations of how fact or myth becomes folklore. In each case, a working formula illustrates the functional difference between myth and folklore. These include the Mosaic account of the Hebrews crossing the Sea of Reeds, Noah and the Great Flood, the Christmas story, Saint Paul's conversion experience, the baptism of Jesus by John, the trip to the temple, the temptations of Jesus, the transfiguration, the Last Supper, and the crucifixion.

Faithlore

Did Jesus and other spokespeople (prophets, poets, judges, and kings) speak in lore, myth, allegory, proverbs, aphorisms, parable, dogma, theophanies, or in other forms and types of language?

These underlying questions have less to do with the nature of Christianity than the nature of folklore. While episodes or types may be counted and placed in a taxonomy, no single episode may be adjudged to be true in terms of actuality.[2]

Folklore, by its very nature, is not empirical. Neither is Christianity. Further, the attempt to ground Christian theology in causation theory has never passed the test of empirical reasoning, nor has it successfully negotiated the so-called proofs for the existence of God.

The following question will likely always remain: should theological speculation be labeled as myth or folklore? The "believing" public will say "neither." For my purpose I prefer to address theology as "faithlore" simply because of the various denotations and connotations of the word "lore" when it is applied to matters of theology.

The historic definitions of both "myth" and "lore" are too numerous for discussion in this chapter. However, as a working principle, I hold that myth often arises from some happenstance occurrence, while folklore is most often an interpretation, elaboration, embellishment, frame, or spin placed upon the myth event.

---

2. As per folklorist Stith Thompson.

In other words, to place an event into an assumed historical frame will often yield myth, after which folklore frequently follows as an interpretation, embellishment, or elaboration of the myth.

> a. Activating Agent: An event, occurrence, or happening.
>
> b. Belief: The activating agent could be adjudged as true. Or, it may be adjudged as myth. Some will claim the Gospel accounts to be both truth (Jesus lived) and myth (but most of the reporting about him is mythological).
>
> c. Consequences: If belief is adjudged as myth or partial myth, there will be interpretation, embellishment, elaboration, or spin about it. This is folklore. (For this ABC methodology, I am indebted to Albert Ellis, inventor of Rational Emotive Behavior Therapy and author of *Growth through Reason*.[3])

The reader may separate for herself/himself what should be labeled at level B (belief) as truth or myth (it is not wrong to admit to an intermingling of truth and myth). However, once we have declared at level B that some part of the written biblical account is myth, we must then proceed to level C and examine the consequences arising out of the mythological part(s) of the belief. As we have pointed out, the ensuing interpretation, embellishment, elaboration, and spin becomes folklore/faithlore.

What is truth?
What is myth?
What is folklore?

The Storyteller's License

A storyteller usually has great license or assumed permission to add, subtract, or fill in otherwise unspoken details. It is no different in the matter of the Gospel writers, editors, and redactors. In the introduction to *The Five Gospels: What Did Jesus Really Say?*,

---

3. Ellis, *Growth through Reason*, 1–14.

3 MYTH, FOLKLORE, AND FAITHLORE

Funk and Hoover point out that any readable text at times requires such editing.[4] They note that Jesus might have said:

> "Let us cross to the other side" (Mark 4:35) [or] "The time is up. God's imperial rule is closing in. Change your ways and put your trust in the good news" (Mark 1:15) . . . To forecast the outcome of his own gospel story and sum up the gospel then being proclaimed in his community, Mark has Jesus say, "The son of Adam is being turned over to his enemies, and they will end up killing him. And three days after he is killed he will rise!" (Mark 4:40).

Funk and Hoover sum up by stating: "As a consequence, we would expect much of the incidental conversation of Jesus in anecdotes to be the creation of the storyteller."[5]

However, the storyteller has no license to create unwarranted text or verbiage. Editorial redacting for grammatical flow is one thing. Inserting new material in order to change the meaning and/or purpose crosses the unseen line. Again we emphasize that lore is embellishment and interpretation, and must not reflect the editor's whim or point of view. If the editor spins his/her own point of view, we can be sure that we are into folklore, not storytelling. On this point, Funk and Hoover point out that "Jesus' characteristic talk was distinctive—it can usually be distinguished from common lore."[6]

Instances of Biblical Folklore

Our first example of fact becoming myth, which turns to folklore, is Moses and the crossing of the Sea of Reeds. In each and every following illustrative reference, we shall return to the questions (levels A, B, and C) of Figure 3.1.

---

4. Funk and Hoover, *Five Gospels*, 29.
5. Funk and Hoover, *Five Gospels*, 29–30.
6. Funk and Hoover, *Five Gospels*, 30.

Suffice it to say that myth seems to subsume folklore and folk belief more readily than vice versa—i.e., compared to myth being subsumed under folklore. A relevant example is the account of Moses leading the children of Israel through the Red Sea (Exod 15:22; Josh 4:23; Ps 136:13; Heb 11:29). Old Testament scholarship shows clearly that the Red Sea did not gush open (as depicted in many pictures and other accounts) to allow the children of Israel to pass between high-rising waves of flooding waters. Scholarship reveals that the myth began with the misidentification of the Red Sea with the Sea of Reeds, a low-lying mushy plain of reeds.[7] When modern preachers and biblical expositors talk about the Exodus from Egypt as being the handiwork of a divine God (theism), they rarely call it either myth or folklore. They call it and treat it as historical fact. Nevertheless, in tale, lore, song, and dance it is often referred to as folklore.

I would submit to the reader that the folklore began with the wrong naming of the Sea of Reeds as the Red Sea. This was a historical event that quickly became myth and then turned to folklore. The folklore resulted from the easy acceptance of oral mis-history.

Noah and the Great Flood

Our second example of fact becoming myth, which turns to folklore, relates to the Great Flood. Using the formula from Figure 3.1, the flood (Gen 6, level A, the activating agent) is the original impetus for the building of the ark. At level B (belief), the reader is privy to God's instructions to build the ark and place on board some of all creatures that draw breath from the air (Gen 6–9).

At this point, the modern reader will most likely label the flood episode, replete with Noah and the ark and the flood, as myth. Once the entire scenario is recognized and labeled as such, the work of folklore begins. Now comes the spin, the embellishment,

---

7. Gehman, *New Westminster Dictionary,* 794; "the sea called by the Hebrews *yam suph* or *sea of reeds.*" The *New Revised Standard Version* allows a footnote to denote Exodus 15:22, Joshua 4:23, and Psalms 136:13 as referring to the Sea of Reeds.

3 MYTH, FOLKLORE, AND FAITHLORE

and the lore about the entire flood event, including the rainbow, the sign of God's covenant with humankind that he (God) shall never again destroy the earth and its air-breathing creatures. There is also the follow-up account of Noah getting drunk as soon as he could grow the fruit of the vine and how, after Noah was completely intoxicated, his sons covered his nakedness.

The Christmas Story

It is a story with several storytellers. Let us look next at the events surrounding the birth of Jesus. We begin with Matthew and Luke. "In those days a decree went out from Emperor Augustus that all the world should be registered . . . Joseph also went from the town of Nazareth in Galilee to Judea, to the city of David called Bethlehem, because he was descended from the house and family of David . . . And in that region there were shepherds living in the fields, keeping watch over their flock by night. (Luke 2:1, 4, 8). We next add to the Lukan account that of Matthew 1:18–25: "Look, the virgin shall conceive and bear a son, and they shall name him Emmanuel, which means 'God with us'" (Matt 1:23).

At this level (level A, the activating agent), we have news of a birth. Let us accept this announcement as truth. However, there is myth connected with it. I don't know about this business of Mary being a virgin, betrothed to Joseph. Nor do I know about connecting this birth with the prophecy in Isaiah. I do know that when conception occurs without sexual intercourse or artificial insemination, it is proclaimed as an attempt to invoke some sort of divine authority. "Therefore the Lord himself will give you a sign. Look, the young woman is with child and shall bear a son, and shall name him Emmanuel" (Isa 7:14). At level B, belief, I shall label the news of the birth event as both truth and myth.

But now let us look at level C, the consequences of the belief. The consequences of the truth at level B have had powerful impact on humankind for over two millennia. But there also seems to be a great amount of myth surrounding the truth. Yes, a baby is born

35

to Mary. The father is speculated to be Joseph, a woodworker. The baby will be a savior of the world.

At level C, the consequences of the myth begin. This is the beginning of folklore (or faithlore). There is no end to it! Throughout the pages of the New Testament, throughout the history of the Eastern and Western church fathers and the various theologians of Christendom, folklore has grown rampant from myth. From the annual school play to the courthouse diorama to the church reenactment, we have a mixture of truth and myth and folklore. Bishop John Spong, writing on the events recorded by Matthew and Luke, states:

> We do both the Bible and human scholarship a grave disservice when we try to literalize and make history out of these interpretative myths, created by the second or third generation of those who were the disciples of this Jesus. No reputable biblical scholar in the world today, Catholic or Protestant, treats these narratives of Matthew and Luke as history. It is time the church said that publicly.[8]

All of the events recorded in Luke 2–4 and Matthew 1–3 need to be submitted to A-B-C methodology.

The Trip to the Temple

The trip to the temple took place when the young adolescent boy stayed behind in Jerusalem, and his parents had to return to find him. Luke has Jesus say, "Why were you searching for me? Did you not know that I must be in my father's house?" (Luke 2:49).

a. Activating Agent: Leaving Jesus behind in the temple.

b. Belief: This appears to be a mythical story.

c. Consequence: Interpretation, embellishment, elaboration, spin, faithlore, and more.

---

8. This quote is taken from a greeting card sent by John Shelby Spong on December 22nd, 2004, entitled 'Meaning of Christmas Myths.'"

3 MYTH, FOLKLORE, AND FAITHLORE

What kind of parent or guardian would travel for three days not knowing where their twelve-year-old was? And furthermore, what child would simply brush off his parent's concern by saying "Why were you searching for me?" (This is lore! It is a clueless child saying a careless and irrational thing.)

The Baptism by John

"And a voice from heaven said, This is my son, the beloved, with whom I am well pleased" (Matt 3:17).

At level B, belief, I would readily adjudge this as myth. The reason I call it myth is that, of the Gospel accounts, only Matthew has a prolonged account of Jesus' baptism. Mark (1:9–11) barely acknowledges the baptism; Luke likewise (3:21–22). We know that Mark wrote the earliest Gospel (ca. AD 65), and that both Matthew and Luke had access to Mark (Mark is usually dated 65–68 CE, Matthew is usually dated 70–85 AD, and Luke is usually dated 75–85 AD).[9] We also know that Matthew wrote primarily for a Jewish audience, and that Luke wrote primarily for a gentile readership.

Matthew's account of Jesus' baptism contains far more information than do Mark or Luke. It would appear that Matthew pushes the lore because he wants to demonstrate to his Jewish readership that Jesus stands squarely within the Jewish Messianic tradition. As such, I must take Matthew's account as lore. It is based on the fact of Jesus' baptism, but nowhere do we have any factual basis for the additional information pertaining to John's statement that Jesus should baptize John, rather than the other way around. Jesus' retort ("Let it be so now; for it is proper for us in this way to fulfill all righteousness") is found only in Matthew 3:13–17. This would be pleasing to Jewish listeners.

---

9. Gehman, *New Westminster Dictionary*, 572, 599, 590.

FAITHLORE

The Temptations (Matt 4:1–11)

He fasted forty days and forty nights, and afterward he was famished. The temptor came and said to him, "If you are the Son of God, command these stones to become loaves of bread." But he answered, "It is written, 'One does not live by bread alone.'"

Then the devil took him to the holy city and placed him on the pinnacle of the temple, saying to him, "If you are the Son of God, throw yourself down, for it is written, 'He will command his angels concerning you'" . . . Jesus said to him, "Again it is written, 'Do not put the Lord your God to the test.'"

Again, the devil took him to a very high mountain and showed him all the kingdoms of the world and their splendor. And he said to him, "All these I will give you, if you will fall down and worship me." Jesus said to him, "Away with you, Satan! For it is written, 'Worship the Lord your God and serve only him.'" (Matt 4:1–11)

At Level A, the precipitating event, this entire passage is myth. Matthew puts words in the mouth of Satan which tempt and seduce Jesus. This passage is not to be found in Mark or Luke or Quelle (the otherwise unnamed source for Jesus' sayings).[10] Paul does not mention it. Generations of Christian believers have participated in the creation of folklore surrounding the temptations of Jesus, even to the point of preaching fodder. The temptations make for great storytelling.

---

10. Funk and Hoover, *Five Gospels*, 12–18. The otherwise-unnamed Q document contains writings about Jesus and his life and teachings. The four-source theory speculates that Mark and Quelle provide the material to which Luke and Matthew have access. Matthew leans on Mark and Quelle and his own private source, M. Luke relies on Mark and Quell, as well as his own private source, L.

3 MYTH, FOLKLORE, AND FAITHLORE

The Transfiguration
(Matt 17:1–13; Mark 9:1–8; Luke 9:28–36)

Here we have a report that Jesus was transfigured (his appearance seemed to change drastically) before Peter, James, and John. "And he was transfigured before them, and his face shone like the sun, and his clothes became dazzling white. Suddenly there appeared to them Moses and Elijah, talking with him" (Matt 17:1–3).

While this episode is also mentioned by Mark and Luke, it likely originates with Matthew, who, as we have seen, appears to be directing his prose toward a Jewish audience. No doubt Matthew considers the episode to be factual. Nevertheless, we must consider that it most likely is one of those stories about Jesus which places him directly into Mosaic thought with Old Testament tales of the prophet Elijah. We can rest assured that such a tale would have had a great impact on Matthew's Jewish audience.

We must conclude at level B, belief, that there is no cause for this episode to be labeled as fact. It is pure Matthean wishful thinking. As such, at level B we consider it myth and proceed to consider at level C the various interpretations, elaborations, embellishments, and spins that have been placed upon this episode.

The Last Supper
(Mark 14:12–25; Matt 26:26–29; Luke 22:7–23)

In its most simple and primary form, the account of the Last Supper in Mark is a basic building block (Mark 14:22–25): "While they were eating, he took a loaf of bread, and after blessing it he broke it, and gave it to them, and said, 'Take; this is my body.' Then he took a cup, and after giving thanks he gave it to them. And all of them drank from it. He said to them, 'This is my blood of the covenant, which is poured out for many. Truly I tell you, I will never again drink of the fruit of the vine until that day when I drink it new in the Kingdom of God.'"

Did this event actually happen? Probably, at least in some form. It would not be unlikely that Jesus ate privately with his disciples, especially the evening prior to the crucifixion. At level A, the precipitating event, was the gathering, according to Mark, in the upper room (Mark 14:12–21). At level B, belief, we must ask if it is truth or myth. We conclude that it is myth. We note that Funk and Hoover consider the Eucharistic passages to be likely additions to the early Markan account, this being easily assimilated by Matthew, Luke, and Quelle.[11]

What are the consequences (level C) of the mythical belief? The consequences are several, and they strongly impact the eucharistic practices of the modern church.

First, we note that the eucharist of the Roman Catholic Church has claimed from earliest times that the bread becomes the actual body of Christ and the wine becomes the actual blood of Christ. This is the belief in transubstantiation.[12] The Lutheran Church holds to the belief that the bread unites "with" the body of Christ and the wine unites "with" the blood of Christ. This is the belief in consubstantiation.[13] Luke 22:19 adds the words "Do this in remembrance of me." This is the basis for the Presbyterian and Reformed traditions using the word "remembrance" in the ritualistic words of the communion service.

The second consequence of the several accounts of the Last Supper is simply the fact that, while the biblical accounts are usually considered authentic, the lore that surrounds the Roman Catholic and Lutheran interpretations remains highly significant

---

11. According to Funk and Hoover, "Mark is the sole source of this story; he is copied by both Matthew and Luke ... nothing in this narrative can be attributed to Jesus; story and words are integral to each other. Since Mark created the narrative in his own words, he undoubtedly also composed the words ascribed to Jesus" (*Five Gospels*, 116).

12. "Transubstantiation: an act or instance of being transubstantiated. The miraculous change by which according to Roman Catholic and Eastern Orthodox dogma the eucharistic elements at their consecration become the body and blood of Christ while keeping only the appearances of bread and wine" (*Merriam-Webster's Collegiate Dictionary: Eleventh Edition*).

13. "Consubstantiation: the actual presence and combination of the body and blood of Christ with the Eucharistic bread and wine according to a teaching associated with Martin Luther" (*Merriam-Webster's Collegiate Dictionary: Eleventh Edition*).

3 MYTH, FOLKLORE, AND FAITHLORE

and much adored in faithlore. Aside from lore surrounding the birth of Jesus and his crucifixion, the traditions surrounding the Last Supper remain the strongest of all Christian faithlore.

Belief In Heaven and Hell: Paul On the Road to Damascus

Our penultimate example of myth becoming folklore arises from the popular belief in hell and heaven. A cursory reading of the North American religious landscape would appear to give evidence that fundamentalist, conservative, and even quasi-liberal believers still hold to a strong sense of hell and/or eternal punishment, as well as a vivid belief in some form of immortality.

I shall now focus on one of the most basic tenets of Christianity, the belief in heaven and hell. In terms of the Christian belief regarding the resurrection of "believers," we refer to 1 Corinthians 15. Paul says emphatically that if Christ did not rise from the dead, our faith or belief in our own resurrection is dead: "For if the dead are not raised, then Christ has not been raised. If Christ has not been raised, your faith is futile and you are still in your sins . . . But in fact Christ has been raised from the dead, the first fruits of those who have died. For since death came through a human being, the resurrection of the dead has also come through a human being, for as all die in Adam, so we will all be made alive in Christ" (15:16–17, 20–22a).[14] (Compare this with the first four theories of atonement in chapter 2).

We must ask, "how does Paul know all this?" The answer is to be found in Paul's conversion experience on the road to Damascus. As the account goes, Paul was suddenly blinded. "He fell to the ground and heard a voice saying to him, 'Saul, Saul, why do you persecute me?' He asked, 'Who are you, Lord?' The reply came, 'I am Jesus, whom you are persecuting. But get up and go into the city and you will be told what you are to do'" (Acts 9:4–6).

The point of this excursus is quite simple: this is the exact moment where the Pauline testament to the resurrected Jesus

---

14. The reader is reminded that the rotten smelling garbage/trash pit outside Jerusalem, the Valley of Hinnon or Gehenna, is often translated as "hell."

began. From here on, Paul is presumed to be the supreme authority, and he is is absolutely convinced that Jesus rose from the dead and that Jesus' followers will do likewise. This is the beginning of the resurrection myth. (Or, if you prefer, this is the beginning of the myth about believers being raised from the dead, a belief upon which streams of folklore have been based.[15])

Christian theism (and later dogma) says that God will raise believers from the dead, just as God has raised Jesus from the dead. (The gospels of Matthew, Mark, Luke, and John were written many years after the reputed words of Paul in 1 Corinthians 15, and thus cannot be used as proof of Paul's argument.[16]) This account serves as a link to the second creation account, Genesis 2:4—4:26, upon which Paul builds his theological doctrine of God, salvation, and damnation. This is obvious because Paul talked about humankind deserving death due to Adam's sin of disobedience.

The folklore growing out of the Pauline conversion experience is paralleled in other non-Christian accounts.[17] As long as humankind chooses sin and disobedience to a theistic deity, there will be no salvation. The entire folkloric drama is based on a sin/salvation platform. Upon this platform Christian theological folklore has flourished, aided and abetted by a three-story worldview. Neither the preaching of the fundamentalist preachers nor the neo-orthodoxy of a Karl Barth or Reinhold Niebuhr has been successful in calling out the Genesis myth, with its popular folklorist ranting about sin and salvation, i.e., the penal substitutionary theory of atonement. As we have seen, even John Calvin was completely taken in by the "punishment for sin" argument.

---

15. Luke is reputed to be the author of Acts.

16. Most biblical scholarship claims that Luke's hand in writing the Acts precedes the writing of the Gospel of Luke. "The Acts should be dated at least before Paul's martyrdom, which took place about A.D. 67 . . . It is written with much artistic power, and supplies the information necessary to explain the rise of Christianity as a universal religion during the 33 years from the death of Christ" (Gehman, *New Westminster Dictionary*, 14).

17. Campbell and Moyers, *Power of Myth*.

3 MYTH, FOLKLORE, AND FAITHLORE

The Crucifixion and Bodily Resurrection of Jesus: the Prime Myth of Christendom

With good reason, Christianity is often referred to as the resurrection faith. Were it not for the reputed resurrection of Jesus of Nazareth from the burial cave with a huge stone placed in front of it (this too, could be myth), there simply would be no basis for the growth and spread of Christianity. Jesus' death would likely have gone unnoticed. In short, there is little doubt about the historicity of Jesus, the man. Whether he was the Son of God or a son of man remains a question for the ages.[18]

The alleged resurrection is another question. Here, as we noted in 1 Corinthians 15, is the essential myth about which much folklore has been promulgated. Again, Paul says, "For if the dead are not raised, then Christ has not been raised. If Christ has not been raised, your faith is futile and you are still in your sins" (15:16–17).

Our basic question is whether Christian theism can legitimately be considered as folklore. My response is quite succinct: yes. It can be considered folklore because it is based on the myth of the resurrection of Jesus. It is also a matter of historical record that no other claim to the empirical truth of theism has ever been established.

If people choose to believe in specific forms of life after death, whether the belief be classified as spiritual, deistic, theistic, transcendent, or immanent, let it be clearly understood that folklore based on myth can never be asserted as empirical knowledge.

None of the above explanations can even begin to explain the seemingly powerful hold the myth and ensuing folklore of sin and salvation has upon the religious world. Why do people yearn to be "saved?" Saved from what? Is it a question of being reunited with family? With often-estranged parents and siblings? Is it a fear of

---

18. In this monumental work *Did Jesus Exist? The Historical Argument for Jesus of Nazareth*, Ehrman makes a strong case for the historical fact of Jesus. This book is a polemic in response to the so-called "mythicists" who claim that the historical Jesus was himself a myth. See also Cooke, "Myth Theory."

punishment? Is it guilt? Is the entire question of faith a matter of seeking inner peace and comfort?[19]

Since my former life and career as a Presbyterian cleric, I can only speculate that believers seem to rejoice in their folkloric beliefs about life after death. My experience was that far too many believers build an impervious shell around their "thinking" mind, shutting out the wisdom bequeathed to us by science and the considered thought of educators, ministers, philosophers, and, yes, folklorists.

Without the interaction of the *sapiens* brain with the infinite realm of imaginative possibilities, we would be a non-culture and a non-society, or at best a culture of Neanderthals or Denisovans. Think of life without Shakespeare, Socrates, Aristotle, Plato, Descartes, Locke, Hume, Berkeley, Bach, Beethoven, Mozart, Handel, Verdi, Puccini, Hammerstein, or Lerner, with no Renaissance, no modern application of physics and the laws of thermodynamics. Take away all machine power, including locomotion and aerodynamics, atomic and hydrogen bombs of destruction (some would readily agree that *sapiens* would be better off without nuclear power). Let us take away the table of minerals and music such as jazz, Broadway, country, and the blues. Truth be told, civilization as we know it is the end result of interaction between *sapiens* and imagination. This is hardly an exaggeration, as without the ability to imagine, the *sapiens* brain would most likely atrophy (see chapter 4).

Indeed, let us ask at last, do we become religious in order to escape responsibility for our own being and behavior? Is the turn to God, folkloric or not, an attempt to shield ourselves from our own folly?

> All human societies recognize powers that are greater than themselves, such as light and dark, sun, storm, and frost; flood and drought; and the growth of the plants on which their lives depend. Investing such powers with spirits that have a recognizably human nature has allowed people to make greater sense of a random and

---

19. Freud, *Future of An Illusion*.

3 MYTH, FOLKLORE, AND FAITHLORE

threatening universe. Propitiating the spirits with offerings and prayers allows their worshippers to feel that they may have a degree of control. At the same time, by seeking the protection of a deity, devotees are able to relinquish responsibility for their own lives to a higher authority. Myths concerning gods and goddesses help to give shape to the powers that are seen to preserve or endanger humanity.[20]

---

20. Cotterell and Storm, *Illustrated Encyclopedia of World Mythology*, 6–7.

4 Constructivism and the Human Brain

The concluding chapter of this book will focus on the activity of the brain of *Homo sapiens* since its inception as a species between 150,000 and 70,000 years ago.

We will consider how it might have come about that humankind came to believe in some sort of god in the first place. We will not assume that the species *Homo sapiens* is hardwired in any sense for belief in deity or a god. We will assume, however, that religious belief developed and matured out of a sense of perceived need.

>What's that you say?
>I'm a solipsist?
>I'm a pantheist?
>I'm a panentheist?
>I'm a gnostic?
>I'm a what? I beg your pardon.

Labels are sometime counterproductive, even dehumanizing. Nevertheless, often they can be helpful in describing objects or people with an exactness and precision of meaning that is otherwise impossible.

Solipsism is the belief that the only reality is the human mind.
Pantheism is the belief that God is all.
Panentheism is the belief that God is in all.

4 CONSTRUCTIVISM AND THE HUMAN BRAIN

Gnosticism is the belief that knowledge, usually spiritual knowledge, is the supreme essence of life.

Constructivism is a term indicating that reality can be known only through the brain because the brain is the agency that enables the human being to invent, create, perceive, and hence construct the world.

Radical Constructivism

Radical constructivism, in its most recent reformulation, has been championed, among others, by Ernst von Glasersfeld and Paul Watzlawick. Jean Piaget is often credited with being the modern champion of constructivism, setting forth the role of the brain in learning theory.

As the reader is well aware, the title of this work is *Faithlore*. Before this term can be adequately dealt with, we must backpedal to the question of constructivism, especially radical constructivism. In this backward journey, we must consider the role and significance of the human brain.

In what are perhaps two of his most concise statements regarding radical constructivism, Glasersfeld says the following:

> For constructivists, all communication and all understanding are a matter of interpretative construction on the part of the experiencing subject ... Radical constructivism, thus, is *radical* because it breaks with convention and develops a theory of knowledge in which knowledge does not reflect an "objective" ontological reality, but exclusively an ordering and organization of a world constituted by our experience.[1]

Immanuel Kant concluded the impossibility of knowing the *a priori* except in the cases of mathematics and physics. He finally confined himself to the world of phenomena, not noumena (the so-called matter of metaphysical reality, which he concluded to be unknowable).

---

1. Watzlawick, *Invented Reality.*

Nevertheless, the unknowable is not necessarily non-existent. It is simply that the *sapiens* mind cannot lay any claim to knowledge regarding the ontological or metaphysical reality. Any and all knowledge regarding the noumena and the so-called ontological reality can only be the result of the activity of the *sapiens* brain that constructs these realities.

Again, let us turn to Glasersfeld:

> Radical constructivism... is an unconventional approach to the problem of knowledge and knowing. It starts from the assumption that knowledge, no matter how it be defined, is in the heads of persons, and that the thinking subject has no alternative but to construct what he or she knows on the basis of his or her own experience. What we make of experience constitutes the only world we consciously live in.[2]

Hence, we see immediately that constructivism is a theory of epistemology. Epistemology concerns itself with how we know something. As such, radical constructivism claims that knowledge is the result of the individual interacting with the environment—both the immediate personal environment and the greater environments of community, city, state, forests, oceans, solar system, galaxies (think the Milky Way), and the entire universe.

The most basic of questions, "how do we know reality?", becomes the focal point of constructivism simply because we cannot ever be certain of what reality is. We may think we know reality, but usually after a series of probing questions we discover, with Locke, Berkeley, and Hume, that reality depends entirely on our perception of reality. While many of us may agree on our alleged perceptions, we still can never be certain of what we think we know; except perhaps, according to Kant, our perceptions related to mathematics and physics. Mathematics and physics qualify for classification as the *a priori* analytic, simply because the predicate is built into the subject—that is to say, the ball is round, wherein roundness (on being a perfect sphere) is an attribute of perfect

---

2. Glasersfeld, *Radical Constructivism*, 1.

ball-ness. This excludes an American football, which is technically not a ball at all because it is not a perfect sphere.

In sum, we use our minds to study and explore the world about us. We do this to acquire knowledge and understanding, via physics, astrophysics, astrobiology, the sciences, etc. This is not constructivism. Constructivism is the activity of the brain, usually unconscious but not exclusively so, that works to invent, create, and construct realities. Constructs treat both the objective and subjective worlds about us, causing us to apprehend and comprehend all of life, but always via the agency of the mind as it seeks to adapt to the challenges of internal and external environments. The end result of constructivism is in how it conditions and prepares the mind to perceive reality. In this sense, constructs both precede and follow our perceptive adaptations.

The Theological Construction

The question remains to be addressed: is God a theistic reality? In other words, is there a monotheistic omnipotent reality that undergirds, creates, sustains, and directs the various parts and persona of the multiverse?

Radical constructivism holds steadfastly to the view that there is not now nor has there ever been any possible way we may know with certainty the truth or falsehood of such a statement. The closest we can come to any viable answer to the question is to study and analyze the constructs that human beings have created or invented over previous millennia. Even thus, the evidence is neither empirical nor scientific for the simple reason that it is anecdotal, depending entirely on the personal experience of individual human beings.

Another way of saying this is that there may be an eternal force we call God, but there is absolutely no way humans can know the objective reality of such a force. The only alternative for *Homo sapiens* is to study the brain and its construction of a god or god force within its own life or life experience. This is the constructivist reality. Your god is the god your brain has invented or created.

How Does It Work? Telling the Tale

Do you remember the days before radio? Few can! There are countries and places far out of the mainstream wherein the populace has not encountered radio. More commonly, there are places wherein television is unknown. I invite you to step back in time when the art of telling tales was the most popular of leisure pastimes.

The one absolutely essential ingredient for becoming involved in storytelling is imagination. Of course, there is an art to good storytelling. Nevertheless, from the listener's perspective, there had to be some willingness to become entranced or caught up in the story. Certainly, with ghost stories, especially around the campfire, it was no fun if people did not lend the storyteller an empathic ear.

In his young adulthood, between 1933 and 1936, Ronald Reagan was employed by radio stations; WOC in Davenport, Iowa; and WHO in Des Moines, Iowa to recreate the play by play of the *Chicago Cubs*. There was an art to this, and Reagan was reportedly good at his craft. At the home field, a cohort programmed the wireless ticker tape play-by-play proceedings from the ballpark. Then, by prior arrangement, Reagan or one of his cohorts would endeavor to dramatize and embellish what he read on the ticker tape. He would use sound effects of all types. Crowd boos. Cheering. The thud of the ball being caught in a leather glove. And, of course, the sound of a bat hitting the ball, a sharp crack of wood on leather. Timing was important, especially judging the amount of time between pitches.

> Ball two. High and outside.
>
> Here's the wind-up. Strike one. A swing and a strong miss, like he wanted to go deep. The pitcher goes to the resin bag.
>
> O.K. He steps on the rubber.
>
> Here's the pitch. [A sharp crack of the bat.] And there's a long fly ball into deep center. He's going back, back, back.

4 CONSTRUCTIVISM AND THE HUMAN BRAIN

He leaps. He got it! He got it ! [Turn up the pre-recorded crowd noise.] What a catch! Unbelievable!

From my own youth, on a rare visit to Idora Park in Youngstown, Ohio, I recall being swept away. I wasn't just hearing the Cleveland Indians baseball announcers Jack Grainy (and maybe Van Patrick). I was watching them set up shop and then carry us through the entire nine innings of reconstructed baseball. Our imaginations allowed us to become totally absorbed in the game. It was real! It was alive! It was exciting!

Of course, if I was not able to go to Idora Park, I would sit at home and listen intently on the radio (no TV back then) to every play, every strikeout, every nuance, as re-created by the announcers. If it was an afternoon game (in the mid-forties, most games were afternoon), I often had my pleasure interrupted because I had to set out on my paper route.

The world of children's books opened many youngsters to the wonders and fantasies of all kinds of literature. Here is the basis for folklore and tales of yore, wherein everything was placed upon the mental ability and agility of the child. No wonder one of the points of observation social workers routinely note when making home visitations related to childcare and welfare is the obvious presence or absence of children's books and drawing/coloring materials (and, of course, creative children's games).

In all of this, we witness the involvement and active participation of the *sapiens* brain. The brain makes it possible for the imagination to incorporate what it is being fed or supplied. The child or youth can become quickly caught up in a reality totally created by spoken, written, and enacted word. Religious stories and accounts are likely subjects of such stories and revelatory accounts, including all manner of the supernatural. Bible stories replete with miracles of nature, healings, resurrections, killings, and massive warfare abound in Christian children's literature. "Jesus loves me this I know, for the Bible tells me so." Oh? And just where and how often and in what context does the Bible tell you so? (Matt 19:14).

The stories of Little Red Riding Hood, Goldilocks, Snow White, Rumpelstiltskin, Hansel and Gretel, and Pinocchio do not quickly leave the mind of the child, to say nothing of Santa Claus and the Easter Bunny. This literature has had great impact on children. In itself, it may be neither good nor bad—my point being that it thrives on the power of imagination because it is the stuff upon which the child's credulous mind will easily seize.

The reader may retort that there is much that is wholesome in the myth and folklore of children's literature. Emphatically, I do not question such a verdict. Nevertheless, it remains in the power of the child's imagination to create, invent, and construct its realities based almost entirely upon impressions absorbed by the child's mind.[3]

The Brain

We have heard so much throughout our lives about the magnificence of the *sapiens* brain that it becomes almost a ho-hum truism. Nevertheless, the truth is far more spectacular than we have been led to believe. It is hard to accept the wanton killing and destruction of any human life when we realize the absolute perfection of this most wondrous product of evolution. And yet, it is in the brain that the desire and impulse to kill initially takes root. This is why neurophysiologists and neurobiologists consider brain study of famous and infamous persons so important.

Let us take a quick highlight tour of our brain. We will enter from the bottom up, so to speak, through the brain stem to the various lobes. The brain stem is that part of the brain that leads into the cerebrum, another name for the entire cavity housing the major part of the brain. The brain stem serves as a conduit encasing nerves and neuro-pathways to the entire lower part of the body, making it possible for us to move arms, legs, fingers, and

---

3. I once criticized a seminary-educated cleric for her children's sermon wherein she talked about Moses leading the Israelites across the Red Sea. In doing so, she enforced the myth that Moses parted the Red Sea by causing a wind to blow back the waves. My criticism was simply that this cleric knew very well this was not the Red Sea, but a marsh known as the Sea of Reeds. Why not at least be honest when dealing with the minds of children (and adults)?

4 CONSTRUCTIVISM AND THE HUMAN BRAIN

toes. The brain stem also encases neuro-pathways to the internal organs that make up parts of the respiratory and digestive systems.

Going upward through the brain stem, we encounter the cerebellum,[4] and then the right and left temporal lobes, so named for the temple area afore and above each side of the ear. Behind the temporal lobes are the parietal lobes.[5] The occipital lobes are in the back part of the cerebrum, and are concerned with vision. Between these sets of lobes are small glands such as the thalamus, hippocampus, and amygdala. The amygdala is the center of the limbic or emotional system. The hippocampus is vital for memory, especially spatial memory. Coming forward, we encounter the huge (by comparison) right and left frontal lobes and prefrontal areas.

When people talk about the right brain and left brain, they are usually referring to the frontal lobes, because this is where we do our thinking. This is where thoughts are joined together in coherent patterns, leading to original constructs of various descriptions. Here we encounter upwards of one hundred billion neurons, and three times that number of synapses, which connect the various neurons.

Each of the lobes throughout the brain is protected on its exterior side by a layer known as the cerebral cortex, a gray, wrinkled covering. When we hear of someone taking a blow to the head, we can picture the brain, with its protective cortex, being shaken up against the skull with a penetrating vibration (this is the action wherein boxers, football players, and other athletes suffer concussions; see Figure 4.1 for a pictorial rendering of the brain[6]).

---

4. "The small brain behind the cerebrum that helps regulate posture, balance, and co-ordination" (Carter, *Human Brain Book*, 243).

5. "The parietal lobe is the top back subdivision of the cerebral cortex, mainly concerned with spatial computation, body orientation, and attention" (Carter, *Human Brain Book*, 246; see also the image on page 28).

6. Lee, Joe. Bloomington, Indiana. Graphic representation. Used by permission.

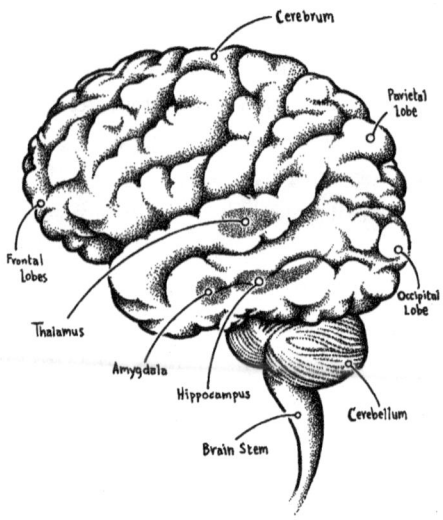

Brain Pix

How Do We Learn?

What we call learning takes place when a snippet of information is transmitted through a neuron to a synapse, and thence to another neuron. This is accomplished through the agency of an electrochemical neurotransmitter.[7] A synapse is "the space typically between an axon of one neuron and a dendrite of another neuron where communication between neurons occurs by release of neurotransmitters. Axon-axon and dendrite-dendrite synapses also exist."[8]

When we think we have learned something, but later discover that we have forgotten that thing, it simply means a neuron connection with a synapse has failed. It bears repeating that the human body contains billions of neurons, and thrice that number of synapses. In our childhood, youth, and early adulthood, we are connecting billions of neurons. Some of these will fail to take hold

---

7. Eagleman, *Brain*, 215.
8. Eagleman, *Brain*, 215.

4 CONSTRUCTIVISM AND THE HUMAN BRAIN

over the long run. Many will strengthen and prove basic to further learning, be it music, law, medicine, philosophy, or the social sciences. With age, some memory is bound to fail. The connections of the neurons sometimes fail. Disease, stroke, and dementia of various kinds often leave the person quite unable to recall recent memory. Predictably, long-term memory is more likely to withstand the ravages of time. According to David Eagleman:

> It feels as though you have direct access to the world through your senses. You can reach out and touch the material of the physical world—like this book or the chair you're sitting on. But this sense of touch is not a direct experience. Although it feels like the touch is happening in your fingers, in fact it's all happening in the mission control center of the brain. It's the same across all your sensory experiences. Seeing isn't happening in your eyes; hearing isn't taking place in your ears; smell isn't happening in your nose. All of your sensory experiences are taking place in storms of activity within the computational material of your brain.[9]

Yes, But How Do We Learn to Believe in God?

The Larue Family

Meet the Larue family. The Larues are a stereotypical North American suburban middle-class, upwardly mobile, family of four. Jane and Howard have been married eighteen years. It is their first marriage. They go to a Ruach temple every Sunday morning. The temple is a religious community of the followers of Ruach, the ever-present, all-powerful, and all-knowing creator of the universe.

Identical twin sons, Robert and Bertram (Rob and Bert), are sixteen years of age. Rob is a musician of some repute. Bert is a star athlete, lettering in both basketball and football. Both boys seem well-adjusted, and enjoy many friends. All four family members enjoy good health. Several years ago, Howard showed signs

---

9. Eagleman, *Brain*, 38–39.

of alcohol abuse, but quickly joined an AA group meeting at the Ruach temple, and was able to pull himself away from possible addiction (he would say that Ruach saved him).

Rob attends weekly services at the Ruach temple under protest, claiming that religious belief is nothing but an invented reality of the mind. Bert, on the other hand, gives daily praise to Ruach for blessing him with athletic prowess and opportunity.

For the Larue family the future looks as bright as the (alleged) promises of Ruach. However, sometimes Rob finds it difficult to keep his mouth shut about the family's attachment to the religion of the Ruach. He sometimes makes "baiting" statements, intended to provoke responses from his mom and dad, and, with greater frequency, his brother Bert. He often says he wonders who or what created the divine Ruach. He says if he is to worship the creator/designer of the universe, he wants to know who or what (force) created Ruach. Whenever Rob talks this way, he knows he can count on pushing his dad's short-temper button, as well as his mother's penchant to take care of everybody by placating, that is, glossing over honest contention by encouraging people to be insincere, pretending to be non-conflicted. This is a type of denial.

Within the Larue family system, there has developed, over many years, a mantra or motto that essentially says, not only does the majority rule, but the majority holds emotional sway over all conflicted issues. A corollary to this belief is that the minority opinion is discounted, and thereby denigrated.

Rob's view of life holds that we can never know what is alleged to be ultimate reality. Rob believes there is reality, but that the only way we can possibly know reality is through the agency of our mind. Our minds continually perceive anything and everything going on outside ourselves. This is the meaning of reality. Because of this belief, Rob freely admits that, when his family and his temple friends talk about Ruach they are, in his opinion, talking about their internalized perception of their sense of reality. In other words, when Rob confronts his father with the statement that he (Rob) believes that Ruach[10] is a construct of his father's

---

10. *Ruach* is Hebrew for the following: to breath, to snuff, to smell, to scent,

4 CONSTRUCTIVISM AND THE HUMAN BRAIN

internal mental processing, Howard becomes defensive and angry. He feels he has been attacked. At this point, Jane usually goes into placating mode by smoothing over the basic dynamics of the argument. This is usually done at Rob's expense, causing feelings of being totally alone in his protestations.[11]

And so the Larue family remains divided. The division pictured here may, in fact, be written large for all humankind to observe and consider in depth. We shall never agree in our constructs, nor in the perceptions that emerge from these constructs. Deconstruction of the theistic premise depends entirely on the willingness of people like Rob Larue to take a firm stand in favor of the constructivist premise. Sometimes such a stand comes at great personal cost.

Many of us are taught religious lore at quite a young age, and the teaching often never stops. Devout belief in God simply continues ad infinitum. Others seem to reach out on their own—kneeling in prayer three times a day or going to "preaching" every Wednesday night and twice on Sundays is bound to have a strong influence on a person's personal theology. Perhaps someone was never religious, but now life has become difficult and terribly stressful, and they reach out for help.

Since about age nine, the vast majority of youngsters know full well the meaning of the finality of death. After that age, we grow up knowing the ever-present possibility of death. For many, there has been a well-cultivated fear of hell and the hereafter. A cursory reading of Saturday newspaper religious pages will serve to illustrate, through sermon titles, the pre-occupation of fundamentalist preachers with the temperature of hell and the coloration of the furniture of heaven.

For many, the prospect of the loss of sons and daughters in warfare, as well as in continuing instances of terror and mindless wanton killing, is absolutely frightening. A glance at the daily obituaries will reveal a goodly portion of folk who, according to

---

to perceive, to pant, an east wind, the breeze, the time of the day, and the breath of life (Ps 135:17; Gen 2:07; 6:17; Acts 17:25).

11. Satir, *Conjoint Family Therapy*.

the grieving loved ones, are now at home in God's holy presence, reuniting with their ancestors, their own fathers and mothers, brothers and sisters. Just recently I read of a three-year-old receiving her angel wings. In my former life, I often wondered what it would be like to talk again with my dad. How I would welcome the opportunity to exchange views on many topics, including his views on politics and sex. I would certainly welcome such a chat. And then the thought would hit me: perhaps Dad is now too busy to talk with me because he is trying to clear things up with his father. And his father with his father.

You've got to be taught to kill, to steal, to cheat, to ridicule, to badger, to bully, to lie, and to commit all manner of evil against your fellow humans. If you are a boy, you've got to be taught how "real boys" are supposed try to "get around" girls. Likewise, you've got to be taught to care, to treasure, to love, to serve, to value, to empathize, to attempt to understand, and to forgive. Somewhere in your journey through life, you may teach yourself to fake orgasms, or to fake emotions such as sadness or joy.

And, of course, you've got to be taught that there is a God in heaven who will protect you if you are good, will forgive you and save you from punishment in "hell" if/when you are bad, and will always watch over you. After all, that's why you worship and pray and sing praises to its holy name!

You've got to be taught to believe all the fairy tales and after-death/future-life nonsense you've been fed by your parents, your aunts and uncles, and even your school teachers. It all happens without our knowing it. Our brain, like all brains, takes command and control of our life and our belief system. We become socialized and acculturated. This is necessary if we are to live as civilized peoples, but the price is sometime quite staggering.

We Learn to Believe in God

Once we learn to believe, it is only a short step to embellishing our belief into a self-created construct; that is, our own personal god construct, our own personal *ruach*.

4 CONSTRUCTIVISM AND THE HUMAN BRAIN

Just don't ask if this constructed god is real. Never doubt the reality of your belief! Of course your god is real! It is absolutely real, dynamic, and alive. But you must not shut your brain off! Ask where this god lives and how this god created everything. Once you have created a firm concept of this external god-force, you may slowly internalize it. Friends, family, and society will help you reinforce the image of this god-force to the point where you actually believe in its power, mercy, love, and acceptance.

Like me, if you ask enough questions and express enough honest doubt, you will hopefully stumble upon the truth of your life. This god, the god of your own learning and construction, lives deeply within the confines of your brain, just waiting for you to rise up and recognize the object of your own creation. Finally, you may one day commit heart, mind, body, and soul to this god figure. Or, you may become a biologist and then do graduate work in brain studies.[12]

L (Language) Interacting with I (Imagination) Equals Lore (L x I = Lore)

Yuval Noah Harari claims that it was the ability of *Homo sapiens* to create language that led to the separation of sapiens from all the other species included in the *homo* genus.

> Language, or *langua*, may be defined as: 1. A body of words and the systems for their use common to a people who are of the same community or nation, the same geographical area, or the same cultural tradition. 2. Language communication by voice in the distinctively human manner, using arbitrary sounds in conventional ways with conventional meanings; speech. 3. The system of linguistic signs or systems considered in the abstract.

---

12. Long before I declared for the Presbyterian ministry, I wrote and delivered a sermon entitled "What Kind of a God?" I raised many relevant issues in that early sermon. It has long since been lost or destroyed, but in it I clearly dwelt on the fact that we construct the kind of god we choose to worship. I truly wish I could re-read that sermon, because within it are the clues as to why I lasted only eleven years as a pastor.

FAITHLORE

> 4. Any set or system of such symbols as used in a more or less uniform fashion by a number of people, who are thus enabled to communicate intelligibly with one another.[13]

Language, of course, has given birth to the profession of language and dialect, and the academic specialty of linguistics in almost all academic institutions of higher learning.

Yuval Harari proceeds to show that when language is applied to *sapiens'* imagination, there is no limit to the thoughts and thought processes of *Homo sapiens*. Once this happened, there was no turning back in the mental evolution of *sapiens*. No other species possessed the ability of language, at least formal spoken language (this is not to deny that hand signals such as "come closer," or "stop," or "over there" were used and understood). Harari points to the fictive reality of imagination by showing how *sapiens* creates banks, corporations, bureaus, institutions of all kinds, even governments that are fictive—that is, they are not "real" in the same sense that your house or your automobile is real.

A fictive reality is often created by law. A fictive reality is "of fiction" or "the production of fiction. Imaginary, feigned."[14] Likewise, if something is a "figment" of the imagination, it is something "formed," something merely imagined or made up in the mind.[15]

Harari states:

> Sapiens have thus been living in a dual reality. On the one hand, the objective reality of rivers, trees and lions; and on the other hand, the imagined reality of gods, nations and corporations. As time went by, the imagined reality became ever more powerful, so that today the very survival of rivers, trees and lions depends on the grace of imagined entities such as the United States and Google.[16]

Language alone does not explain folklore or lore. But when language is applied to imagination, there springs forth an entirely

---

13. *Webster's New World College Dictionary* (3rd edition).
14. *Webster's New World College Dictionary* (3rd edition).
15. *Webster's New World College Dictionary* (3rd edition).
16. Harari, *Sapiens*, 32.

4 CONSTRUCTIVISM AND THE HUMAN BRAIN

new realm of thought: We call this "lore."[17] *Webster's New World College Dictionary* (3rd edition) defines imagination as

> 1a) the act or power of forming mental images of what is not actually present; 1b) the act or power of creating mental images of what has never been actually experienced, or of creating new images or ideas by combining previous experiences; creative power; 2. anything imagined, mental image, creation of the mind, fancy; 3. a foolish notion; 4. the ability to understand and appropriate imaginative creations of others, esp. works of art and literature; 5. resourcefulness in dealing with new or unusual experiences; 6. (obs) an evil plan or scheme.[18]

Folklore, faithlore, or "lore" is the result of *sapiens*' brain power and mental capacity to reach into the heretofore unknown and make assumptions, create as-yet-unknown entities, and formulate principles of ownership, trade, and principles of cooperation never before thought to be possible.

By the time of Abraham (ca. 2000 BCE), Isaac, and Jacob, there was believed to be a transcendent monotheistic God who not only created the earth and the stars, but also was believed to control the activities of human creatures. In other lands and cultures, there were other religious figures and figments of imagination who allegedly wielded power and control over the daily affairs of men.[19] One need only study the records of the mythical gods of Egypt, Mesopotamia, and the Vikings to see how *sapiens*' brain power became imaginative and all-controlling.[20] When we add to these the tribes of Africa, the kingdoms of Eurasia and the Arabians, and the beliefs of the Micronesians and Melanesian, we begin to understand how *sapiens* each invented their own reality.

---

17. Harari, *Sapiens*, 20–39.
18. *Webster's New World College Dictionary* (3rd edition).
19. Campbell and Moyers, *Power of Myth*.
20. Cotterell and Storm, *Illustrated Encyclopedia of World Mythology*.

Faithlore

Did Jesus and other spokespeople (prophets, poets, judges, and kings) speak in lore, myth, allegory, proverbs, aphorisms, parable, dogma, or theophanies, or in other forms and types of language?

These underlying questions have less to do with the nature of Christianity than the nature of folklore. While episodes or types may be counted and placed in a taxonomy, no single episode may be adjudged to be true in terms of actuality. Folklore, by its very nature, is not empirical. Neither is Christianity. Further, the attempt to ground Christian theology in causation theory has never passed the test of empirical reasoning, nor has it successfully negotiated the so-called proofs for the existence of God.[21]

The following question will likely always remain: should theological speculation be labeled as myth or folklore? The "believing" public will say, "neither." For my purpose, I prefer to address theology as "faithlore" simply because of the various denotations and connotations of the word "lore."

The historic definitions of both "myth" and "lore" are too numerous for discussion in this chapter. However, as we have seen, our working principle holds that myth often arises from some happenstance occurrence, while folklore is most often an interpretation, elaboration, embellishment, frame, or spin placed upon the myth event. In other words, to place an event into an assumed historical frame will often yield myth, after which folklore frequently follows as an interpretation, embellishment, elaboration, or spin of the myth.

The Brain As Inventor of Reality

The final point of this chapter is often the most difficult for readers, students, and believers to understand and accept. It is the entire thrust of Eagleman's chapter 2: "What Is Reality?"

---

21. One should pause to credit philosopher David Hume for his break with Christian dogma, as well as philosopher Immanuel Kant for his failed attempt to use reason to establish the existence of God in his *Critique of Pure Reason*.

4 CONSTRUCTIVISM AND THE HUMAN BRAIN

> Your brain serves up a narrative—and each of us believes whatever narrative it tells . . .
>
> Despite the feeling that we're directly experiencing the world out there, our reality is ultimately built in the dark, in a foreign language of electrochemical signals. The activity churning across vast neural networks gets turned into your story of this, your private experience of the world . . .
>
> With seven billion human brains wandering the planet (and trillions of animal brains), there's no single version of reality. Each brain carries its own truth.
>
> So what is reality? It's like a television show that only you can see, and you can't turn it off. The good news is that it happens to be broadcasting the most interesting show you could ask for: edited, personalized, and presented just for you.[22]

In summary, we need to be clear: constructivism does not deny the existence of a reality that exists outside the bounds of the human self—that is, an objective reality outside the human brain. However, constructivism, in liege with the *sapiens* brain, maintains that the only approximation to our knowing reality is through the intervening agency of the human brain. As this concerns our personal theology, the only god we ever know is the god we have invented or constructed. Usually it is a god that is, in some way, a direct reflection of what we have learned to love or what we have learned to rebel against.

We conclude this small book by reasserting the pivotal role and function of the *sapiens* brain in the construction of reality, even including the ontological reality of the existence of God. Make no mistake about it, the god that has been the subject of our construction and invention is none other than the god each of us has previously been taught. As such it is faithlore.

---

22. Eagleman, *Brain*, 38–39.

Conclusion

Fear—Punishment—Security—Comfort—Reunion—Morality—Meaning—Purpose—Design

This is what it seems to be all about. These are the historic motivators. Endless articles and polls and surveys indicate with consistent repetition that the prime motivating factors leading people to belief and faith in God are: 1) fear of punishment in some sort of afterlife; 2) desire for comfort and security in this life where one is free from physical and mental pain and suffering; 3) anticipation of some sort of after-death reunion with one's mate, children, parents, and other kin; 4) the belief that, without God, there would be no basis for moral behavior—that is, no real motivation to be a "good" or to be ethical person; 5) without God, there would be no meaning to human existence, no purpose in life; 6) the need to know and believe that the earth is designed, created, and sustained by a supernatural omnipotent force who (which) is always in control.

There are other reasons, but most are corollaries or derivatives of the above. Many people, of course, will protest that life without God is empty. Many will say that folklore and faithlore take away hope. I will not deny that, without a god-force, there will be no hope of physical or spiritual reunion with kin in an afterlife, or that refusal to believe in a god-force cancels out the idea of God as healer. Concerning this last point, healing and recovery from disease and injury, mind and nature can still be strong healing

CONCLUSION

forces, even stronger than the imagined force and power of a fictionalized god.

Not one of the above listed reasons for belief in God can bring about the reality it purports. Believing in a hereafter in which we can be reunited with kin does not make it so. Wishful thinking is no substitute for down-to-earth honesty about the meaning of death as the end of existence. Turning to God for healing is hardly a medical plan. Better to resign yourself to the healing forces of nature than the hope for divine intervention. Since when does belief in some kind of providential meaning for your life relieve you of the responsibility to define for yourself the meaning and purpose of your own existence? And if you need a god figure to give you impetus and motivation to live a moral and ethical life, you certainly belie your own lack of mind-felt and heartfelt resolve to do right for the sake of the right, and for the sake of your responsibility and your accountability to your fellow man, and to yourself. And if it is your need for your own comfort and security that impel you to believe in a heavenly peace and security, then perhaps you should investigate the reasons you wish to remain inside a womb of magical creation.

The question (perhaps the ultimate question) is whether or not a belief you know in your mind to be untrue (that is, a belief that you know to be without fact or empirical foundation, beyond reason or logical validity) can give you peace and comfort? In the final analysis, will your heart accept what your mind rejects? Is it possible for your heart to accept what you know to be untrue? Is this not the greatest lie of all? To deceive yourself?

The reader always has the ultimate word. The writer's last word is only penultimate. Nevertheless, when it comes to the question of lore, especially on the subject of the effect of lore on matters of faith and the existence of a theistic god, the god of revealed theology, every *Homo sapiens* has the same option. We can choose to embrace a God reputed to be Designer, Creator, and Sustainer of all life, galaxies, and universes, and who serves as your personal Savior, or we can choose to adapt our personal belief system to the principles and tenets of known human knowledge, understanding full well the lore undergirding and surrounding the facts of our existence.

Without begging the question, it is impossible to prove any god hypothesis. We cannot assume a premise to be true and then invoke the use of that premise as proof of itself. Lore, especially faithlore, does not assume truth. It does not invoke itself in order to prove itself. Faithlore is simply noting the characteristics surrounding and underlying a belief or a phenomenon. As such, faithlore is an invented reality that, when we believe it and invest in it, sometimes makes us feel better about ourselves and about life.

Appendix I: Need Theory

Why Do We Persist in Self-Deception? Why Do We Believe What We Believe?

A complete answer to the question above would require a review of literature covering the latest and the oldest experimental protocols in the fields of both psychology and philosophy. Out of all the available hypotheses and theories, I have chosen an old theory that is no longer in fashion. The Abraham Maslow theory of deficit needs is a straightforward prepotent[1] theory claiming that we all have two basic categories of needs. Some of these needs, such as the need for self-fulfillment and self-actualization, Maslow labels our "being" needs. These can really only be satisfied after our "deficit" needs have been tended to and reasonably satisfied. Deficit needs are four in number: physical needs; safety needs, including both physical safety and psycho-emotional safety; love needs, both perceived and unperceived; and esteem needs, both perceived and unperceived.

Physical needs include food, clothing, and shelter. Safety needs include physical safety, such as protection from enemies and dangers of any kind to one's physical selfhood, as well as mental safety in the presence of threats to one's well-being as a rational and mentally competent person. These threats to one's mental well-being may require defense mechanisms and safety devices of

---

1. Maslow claims that needs are prepotent when more primary needs assert themselves to such a point that it is extremely difficult to move forward until a strong measure of the prior need is met.

a highly sophisticated nature. Love needs—not necessarily sexual love—include the valuation one feels both as a past experience and as an ongoing present reality. These lead to our feelings of self-worth and self-esteem. Esteem needs include self-valuation and valuation from others. These needs include how others see us and how they perceive our worth and importance, at least to a minimum of positive regard.

When a strong measure of the totality of our deficit needs are fulfilled we are then, and only then, somewhat free to pursue our "being" needs.[2] I say "somewhat" because few of us, if any, are so completely fulfilled in the basic need of self esteem that we can waltz merrily through life having fulfilled all of our deficit needs all of the time. It is common to suffer setbacks and times of retrenchment in the quest for deficit-need fulfillment.

In the light of Maslow's deficit-need theory I propose that religion, theology, and the pursuit of God and godly interactions and commandments are endeavors that fall mostly into Maslow's deficit-need categories of the need for self-esteem and the need for love.

This is to say, the answer to our question about why we believe what we believe is that our pursuit to be free from fear, to be free from the threat of divine punishment, to be able to have an external basis for being a moral and good person, to have a clear meaning for one's existence and a purpose in daily life, and to be able to know that God or a god force designed and created the entire universe—all of these are the needs people wish for fulfillment. In other words, we believe because we need to. Or, at least we think we need to!

Such is my rendition of the need theory of belief. In other words, people come to believe that they need satisfaction and fulfillment of every one of the needs listed before. They have these need deficits flaunted in front of them almost every Sunday morning, and sometimes at prayer services on Wednesday nights. They internalize the fact of their own human weakness and depravity. They confess their so-called sins in order to prepare for the divine

---

2. Maslow, *Toward A Psychology of Being*.

forgiveness they believe is certain to follow. They come to the belief that they are, by nature, unworthy of God's grace and that, by faith, good works, repentance, and penance, they will be enabled to be numbered amongst God's elect on earth and in the heavenly day of judgment. All of this is true for Christians, especially evangelical, conservative, fundamentalist believers, as well as for many of the Muslim and Jewish persuasions. The dynamics of the need theory are the same for almost all the theistic religions.

Underneath all of this is a single horrendous belief. The underlying belief is that I am too weak and too impotent to fill these needs on my own for myself. This is why we deceive ourselves into believing the longing of our hearts, in spite of the fact that our minds tell us that none of it is true in any literal sense. We deceive ourselves because we want to feel safe. We want to be deceived. We want to believe the lore that we have been taught. It feels right! If we believe and do the right things, God will take care of me.

In the overall picture, our needs, however we perceive them, give rise to our beliefs. Our beliefs, being the product of assimilation and accommodation, give rise to our constructs. As we have seen, our constructs determine what and how we perceive. Our perceptions become our reality.

Chapter 4 focused on the activity of the brain of *Homo sapiens* since its inception as a species between 250,000 and 150,000 years ago. We have considered how it might have come about that humankind came to believe in some sort of god in the first place. We have not assumed that the *Homo sapiens* species is hardwired in any sense for belief in a deity or god. We have assumed, however, that religious belief developed and matured out of a sense of perceived need.

I originally intended this book for devout Christian believers who never had the chance I had to attend a Christian theological seminary. Unless and until local ministers seek to educate their congregants, at least along some of the famous theological lines as suggested here, there remains little hope for positive change. Who was Jesus the man? As we have seen, Albert Schweitzer studied seventy different "lives of Jesus" written by theologians and scholars during the eighteenth and nineteenth centuries. In this volume, chapter 1 dealt in detail with the consensus of Schweitzer's findings. Further, as chapter 2 illustrated, since early eastern and western times there have been at least five (probably more which were melded and combined) theories of the atonement concerning how God brought about the saving reconciliation between man and God. Today, one theory seems to have won the day, and this is the theory promulgated by John Calvin and the Reformers known as the penal substitutionary theory of atonement, the favorite theory of pulpit pounders and bible thumpers in twenty-first-century America. Rarely do we hear a serious exposition of the exemplar (or moral balance) theory, which seeks to explain the importance of Jesus in a way that makes sense to modern men and women.

For a twenty-first-century view of the Old and New Testaments, we need to have some understanding of both hermeneutics and exegesis. Much of this can be taught from the pulpit unless the pastor or preacher is determined to patronize his/her congregants by talking down to them, or otherwise manipulating them for his/her personal gain.

The underlying thesis of this work is that the Christian faith of three centuries has become a type of folklore—or "faithlore," as I have dubbed it—without form or content beyond prescriptions about treating people fairly and not being prejudiced. Alternatively, it has been my purpose to show how the human brain constructs reality, producing a robust faith that does justice to the radical teachings of Jesus regarding how we may choose to live our daily lives.

In truth, there can be no honest theological prescription until we realize what the philosopher David Hume realized long ago: our perceptions of reality become our reality whether we like it or not, and there is no such thing as objective reality. This means that all talk of faith is "faithlore"; devoid of historical content, but not necessarily of human meaning.[3]

---

3. Newberg et al., *Why We Believe*.

Appendix II: American Civil Religion

The *American Civil Religion* pushes for expression at public events, including especially July Fourth, Memorial Day, and Veterans Day remembrances. We often hear expressions of American Civil Religion on radio and TV sporting events. I recently was reassured that "the young man's recently deceased grandfather must surely have been proud as he watched the grandson's spectacular slam dunk." This is what Elaide is referring to when he says "the majority of the irreligious still behave religiously, even though they are not aware of the fact. But the modern man who feels and claims that he is nonreligious still retains a large stock of camouflaged myths and degenerated rituals."[1]

Why do baseball players cross themselves before going up to bat? Why do football players point upward to heaven after scoring a touchdown? Is this not folkloric behavior? This is Americana and it is religious folklore.[2] It is this culturally accumulated camouflaged myth and degenerated ritual that passes as the folklore of our discussion. Rob Boston, writing in *The Humanist*, speaks of Ceremonial Deism:

---

1. Elaide, *Sacred and the Profane*, 204

2. The genuine belief that the deceased watched mortals, especially their descendants, from portals in heaven was perhaps most popular in the nineteenth century. This gave birth to the myth. The myth has now given content to the folklore about deceased people casting their gaze and their constant attention upon the behavior of their descendants.

Today, civil religion is a constant reminder to nonbelievers, agnostics, skeptics, and polytheists that their government believes the following: there is one God. It is a good thing to trust in this God. Real Americans do that. You should too... This isn't harmless. It is not mere ceremony. It's a violation of the fundamental right of conscience. Just once, it would be nice to hear a court acknowledge that obvious fact.[3]

Today, in the obituary section of my local newspaper, I was reminded several times that the decedent was now at home with the angels. I believe the overwhelming motivating force that drives and draws the masses into so-called religious expression is the need for hope, comfort, and reassurance, especially the reassurance of some form of life after death.

A good amount of religious talk is certainly not biblical. The Good Samaritan is still praised, although with no direct reference that the Samaritan was hated by those to whom he dispensed aid, medication, and housing. Today, we may think of him as a Palestinian Muslim reaching out to help a member of the hated Jewish Parliament, the Kenesset.

The Golden Rule is proclaimed as though it was authentic Jesus material, when in truth it is a timely relic from religions and cultures past. As mentioned in the text, it appears as part of the Sermon on the Mount in Matthew 7:12, and the Sermon on the Plain in Luke 6:31.[4]

---

3. Boston, "Not-So-Civil Religion," 37.

4. It can be found in negative form in the Tobit (4:15): "What you hate, don't do to someone else." Rabbi Hillel, a Judean rabbi who is reputed to have been a contemporary of Jesus, is supposed to have said, "What you hate, don't do to another. That's the law in a nutshell, everything else is commentary... The golden rule appears in one form or another in ancient texts, Buddhism, Taoism, and Zoroastrianism. It was an important facet of the teaching of Confucius and Laozi in ancient China, as well as in India, Egypt and Greece" (Crosby, *Aftermath*, 114–15).

APPENDIX II: AMERICAN CIVIL RELIGION

Mythological accounts of alleged floods give rise to folklore,[5] as well as creation stories and accounts.[6] The "fallen" estate of humankind, as depicted in the second of the two Genesis creation stories (Gen 1:1—2:4a and 2:1—4:25),[7] continues to command allegiance amongst conservative evangelicals and fundamentalists to this day.

And, of course, the whole concept of hell and punishment after death is multicultural and folkloric to the core. From Saint Peter jokes to rabbi/priest/minister jokes, we participate in the folklore of our American Civil Religion. Of course we don't take it seriously! Do we? To the contrary—we do, in fact, take it seriously. This is what makes it faithlore.

Myth, in itself, is a profound subject. Myth may be constructive, or it may be destructive. While myth is not by definition truth, it may become a vehicle of truth or a means by which truth is conveyed. Since even a simple definition of myth may take hundreds of pages, I have chosen to quote *Merriam Webster's Collegiate Dictionary*: "a traditional story of ostensibly historical events that serves to unfold part of the world view of a people or explain a practice, belief, or natural phenomenon."[8] This definition embraces the concept of a traditional *story* of ostensibly *historical* events that "unfolds" or *explains* part of the worldview (religion) of a people while endeavoring to explain some *practice*, belief, or natural happening/event.

As creatures who are benefactors of the greatest miracle known to *Homo sapiens*, the human brain, we need to appreciate all manner of faithlore and determine how best we can incorporate

---

5. Cotterell and Storm, *Illustrated Encyclopedia Of World Mythology*, 276–77.

6. Cotterell and Storm, *Illustrated Encyclopedia Of World Mythology*, especially the image on page 444.

7. The first creation story is the so-called Seven-Day Account of Creation (Gen 1:1—2:4a). The second account, in Genesis 2:4—4:26, is the account wherein woman was created from one of Adam's ribs, and the serpent persuades Eve to give Adam a bite (or several) of the fruit (3:12–14), ending in Adam and Eve being expelled from the Garden of Eden.

8. *Merriam-Webster's Collegiate Dictionary: Eleventh Edition*, 822.

its numerous lessons into a working belief system that celebrates life with passion, peace, moral integrity, and dignity. It behooves us all to realize how powerful and influential ceremonial deism is in our culture. Indeed, it is faithlore without careful analysis.

Appendix III: Cosmological Evolution and Descent of Sapiens
(a recapitualization)

According to the *National Geographic Society*, there may be as many as a hundred billion galaxies. All of them are the result of the alleged Big Bang explosion, which happened ca. eleven to fifteen billion years ago.[1] Chris Impey narrows it down: "All life in the universe shares the kinship of a birth 13.7 billion years ago."[2] Impey goes on to number the galaxies as being circa sixty million. He states: "The number of stars contained in those galaxies is 10^{22}, or ten thousand billion billion."[3]

Somewhere around the epoch of the Cambrian explosion, some 542 million years ago, there began the earliest stages of the development of living organisms. However, the ascent of man, for our purposes, begins with Lucy.

Richard Dawkins states that

> the common ancestor we share with chimpanzees lived about six million years ago or a bit earlier, so let's split the difference and look at some three-million-year-old fossils. The most famous fossil of this vintage is "Lucy,"

---

1. The National Geographic Society. *The Universe*. A product of *Move On National Geographic Maps and Products*. Washington, DC: 2000; repr., 2010. Text by Stephan P. Maran.

2. Impey, *Living Cosmos*, 51.

3. Impey, *Living Cosmos*, 35.

classified by her discoverer in Ethiopia, Donald Johanson, as *Australopithecus afarensis* . . . Lucy's skeleton is complete enough to suggest that she walked upright on the ground . . . The conclusion from studies of Lucy and her kind is that they had brains about the same size as chimpanzees' but, unlike chimpanzees, they walked upright on their hind legs, as we do . . . It seems quite likely that the species we call *Australopithecus afarensis*—Lucy's species—included our ancestors of three million years ago.[4]

We now go from Lucy, at three million years ago, to the first known *Homo sapiens*. Where and when did *Homo sapiens* enter the equation? In other words, where and when did we enter the picture?[5]

East Africa appears to be the oldest site for the starting point of the evolution of *Homo sapiens*. Edmund Russell claims "the *genus* to which *sapiens* belongs at nearly seven million years ago and species *Homo sapiens* at about 250,000 years ago."[6] Chris Impey sets a *sapiens* date of 150,000 years ago. He claims *Homo sapiens* separated from chimpanzees ca. four million years ago.[7] As noted above, in 2018, it was announced that a *sapiens* upper jawbone was discovered in Misliya Cave, a site in Israel. The finding suggests that modern humans left Africa at least fifty thousand years earlier than previously thought.

Who is closest to reality? Impey says that *Homo sapiens* first evolved 150,000 years ago, while Russell believes it was 250,000 years. In truth, it is not a question of right or wrong, but of scientific calculation after careful definition of terms and boundaries. For our purposes, the arithmetic mean (200,000) of the above dates serves as a reasonable compromise. This means, in terms of more

---

4. Dawkins, *Greatest Show On Earth*, 188–89.

5. Rice, "Oldest Human Fossil," https://www.usatoday.com/story/tech/science/2018/01/25/scientists-discover-oldest-human-fossil-outside-africa/1066138001/. See also Fleur, "In Cave in Israel," https://www.nytimes.com/2018/01/25/science/jawbone-fossil-israel.html.

6. Russell, *Evolutionary History*, 57.

7. Impey, *Living Cosmos*, 180.

APPENDIX III: COSMOLOGICAL EVOLUTION AND DESCENT OF SAPIENS

recent evolutionary history, that as a defined genus (*Homo*) and species (*sapiens*) we are approximately 150,000–250,000 years old.

Our present (right this minute) brains and our ability to think and reason about what we have just read is the product of some eighty-six (or so) billion neurons and millions and millions of synapses in the evolution and maturation of the *sapiens* brain.

Bibliography

Aulen, Gustaf. *Christus Victor*. Eugene, OR: Wipf & Stock, 2003.
Barker, Dan. *Godless: How An Evangelical Preacher Became One of America's Leading Atheists*. Berkeley: Ulysses, 2008.
Bettenson, Henry. *Documents of the Christian Church*. Oxford: Oxford University Press, 1943.
Boston, Rob. "Not So Civil Religion: The Long Running Fraud of 'Ceremonial Design.'" *The Humanist*, February 28, 2018. https://thehumanist.com/magazine/march-april-2018/church-state/not-civil-religion-long-running-fraud-ceremonial-deism.
Brunvand, Jan Harold. *The Study of American Folklore: An Introduction*. 4th ed. New York: Norton, 1998.
Calvin, John. *The Institutes of the Christian Religion*. Philadelphia: Westminster, 1536.
Carter, Rita. *The Human Brain Book*. New York: DK, 2009.
Campbell, Joseph, and Bill Moyers. *The Power of Myth*. New York: Random House, 1991.
Clements, Keith, ed. *Friedrich Schleiermacher: Pioneer of Modern Theology*. The Making of Modern Theology Series. Minneapolis, MN: Fortress, 1991.
Cooke, Bill. "It's Time To Put the Myth Theory of Jesus Aside." *Free Inquiry* 38:2 (Feb/March 2018) 26–29.
Cotterell, Arthur, and Rachel Storm. *The Illustrated Encyclopedia of World Mythology*. New York: Metro, 2011.
Crosby, John F. *Aftermath: Surviving the Loss of God*. New York: Algora, 2013.
———. *The Flipside of Godspeak: Theism As Constructed Reality*. Eugene, OR: Wipf & Stock, 2007.
Dawkins, Richard. *The Greatest Show On Earth: The Evidence For Evolution*. New York: Free Press, 2009.
Eagleman, David. *The Brain: The Story of You*. New York: Pantheon, 2015.
Ehrman, Bart D. *Jesus: Apocalyptic Prophet of the New Millennium*. Oxford: Oxford University Press, 1999.

BIBLIOGRAPHY

———. *Did Jesus Exist? The Historical Argument for Jesus of Nazareth*. New York: HarperOne, 2012.
Eliade, Mircea. *The Sacred and the Profane: The Nature of Religion*. Translated from the French by Willard R. Trask. Orlando, FL: Harcourt, 1957.
Ellis, Albert. *Growth through Reason*. Palo Alto, CA: Science and Behavior, 1971.
Faber, M. D. *The Psychological Roots of Religious Belief: Searching for Angels and the Parent God*. Amherst, NY: Prometheus, 2004.
Fleur, Nicholas St. "In Cave in Israel, Scientists Find Jawbone Fossil From Oldest Modern Human Out of Africa." *New York Times*, January 25, 2018. https://www.nytimes.com/2018/01/25/science/jawbone-fossil-israel.html.
Freud, Sigmund. *The Future of An Illusion*. New York: Anchor, 1964.
Funk, Robert W., and Roy W. Hoover. *The Five Gospels: What Did Jesus Really Say?* New York: Macmillan, 1993.
Gehman, Henry Snyder. *The New Westminster Dictionary of the Bible*. Philadelphia: Westminster, 1970.
Glasersfeld, Ernst von. *Radical Constructivism: A Way of Knowing and Learning*. New York: Routledge-Falmer, 1995.
Grinstead, L. W. *A Short History of the Doctrine of the Atonement*. London: Forgotten, 2015.
Harari, Yuval Noah. *Sapiens: A Brief History of Humankind*. New York: HarperCollins, 2015.
Hume, David. *Dialogues Concerning Natural Religion*. Barnes and Noble Library of Essential Reading. New York: Barnes and Noble, 1779.
———. *A Treatise Of Human Nature*. Barnes and Noble Library of Essential Reading. New York: Barnes and Noble, 2005.
Impey, Chris. *The Living Cosmos: Our Search For Life In The Universe*. New York: Cambridge University Press, 2007.
James, William. "The Varieties of Religious Experience." https://www.giffordlectures.org/lectures/varieties-religious-experience.
Kant, Immanuel. *Critique of Pure Reason*. Barnes and Noble Library of Essential Reading. New York: Barnes and Noble, 2004.
Luther, Martin. "A Mighty Fortress Is Our God." In *The Hymnbook*, edited by David Hugh Jones, n.p. Philadelphia: Westminster, 1955.
Manson, T. W. *The Teaching of Jesus In Its Form and Content*. Cambridge: Cambridge University Press, 1967.
Maslow, Abraham. *Toward A Psychology of Being*. Princeton, NJ: Nostrand, 1962.
Newberg, Andrew, and Mark Robert Waldman. *Why We Believe What We Believe*. New York: Free, 2006.
Paley, William. *Natural Theology: On The Evidences of the Existence and Attributes of the Deity, Collected from the Appearances of Nature*. Boston: Gould and Lincoln, 1960.
Rice, Doyle. "Scientists Discover Oldest Human Fossil Outside of Africa." *USA Today*, January 26, 2018. https://www.usatoday.com/story/tech/

science/2018/01/25/scientists-discover-oldest-human-fossil-outside-africa/1066138001/.
Russell, Edmund. *Evolutionary History: Using History and Biology To Understand Life On Earth*. Cambridge: Cambridge University Press, 2011.
Satir, Virginia. *Conjoint Family Therapy: A Guide To Theory and Technique*. Palo Alto: Science and Behavior, 1967.
Schweitzer, Albert. *The Quest of the Historical Jesus: A Critical Study of Its Progress From Reimarus to Wrede*. Translated by W. Montgomery. Mineola, NY: Dover, 2005.
Strauss, David Friedrich. *The Life of Jesus, Critically Examined*. Translated by George Elliot. 1st English edition. New York: Cosimo, 2008.
Watts, Isaac. "When I Survey The Wondrous Cross." In *The Hymnbook*, edited by David Hugh Jones, 198. Philadelphia: Westminster, 1955.
Watzlawick, Paul. *The Invented Reality: How Do We Know What We Believe We Know? (Contributions To Constructivism)*. New York: Norton, 1984.

www.ingramcontent.com/pod-product-compliance
Lightning Source LLC
Chambersburg PA
CBHW070323100426
42743CB00011B/2532